WeightWatchers®

Grill It!

150 Flex & Core Plan Recipes

Sizzling Steaks, Burgers, Salads, Pizzas,
Barbecued Chicken, even Desserts

CORE PLAN RECIPE

 SPICY

 NO COOK

 20 MINUTES OR LESS

 VEGETARIAN

A WORD ABOUT WEIGHT WATCHERS

Since 1963, Weight Watchers has grown from a handful of members to millions of enrollments annually. Today Weight Watchers is recognized as the leading name in safe and sensible weight control. Weight Watchers members are a diverse group, from youths to senior citizens, attending meetings virtually around the globe. Weight-loss and weight-management results vary by individual, but we recommend that you attend Weight Watchers meetings, follow the Weight Watchers food plan, and participate in regular physical activity. For the Weight Watchers meeting nearest you, call 800-651-6000. Also, visit us at our Web site, **WeightWatchers.com**, or look for *Weight Watchers* Magazine at your newsstand or in your meeting room.

CHARRED BANANAS WITH
SWEET LIME SAUCE, PAGE 212

WEIGHT WATCHERS PUBLISHING GROUP

CREATIVE AND EDITORIAL DIRECTOR	**NANCY GAGLIARDI**
ART DIRECTOR	**ED MELNITSKY**
PRODUCTION MANAGER	**ALAN BIEDERMAN**
ASSOCIATE ART DIRECTOR	**JENNIFER BOWLES**
OFFICE MANAGER AND PUBLISHING ASSISTANT	**JENNY LABOY-BRACE**
EDITOR	**EILEEN RUNYAN**
RECIPE EDITOR	**PAMELA THOMAS**
NUTRITION CONSULTANT	**PATTY SANTELLI**
PHOTOGRAPHER	**DASHA WRIGHT**
FOOD STYLIST	**MICHAEL PEDERSON**
PROP STYLIST	**CATHY COOK**
DESIGN/PRODUCTION	**SHARON ENG**

ON THE COVER: Herbed Beef Burgers, page 45

ABOUT OUR RECIPES

We make every effort to ensure that you will have success with our recipes. For best results and for nutritional accuracy, please keep these guidelines in mind:

- Recipes in this book have been developed for Weight Watchers members who are following either the **Core Plan** or the **Flex Plan** on the TurnAround™ program. All **Core Plan** recipes are marked with our **Core Plan** recipe icon ☑. We include *POINTS*® values so you can use any of the recipes if you are following the **Flex Plan** on the program. *POINTS* values are assigned based on calories, fat (grams), and fiber (grams) provided for a serving size of a recipe.

- All recipes feature approximate nutritional information; our recipes are analyzed for Calories (Cal), Total Fat (Fat), Saturated Fat (Sat Fat), Trans Fat (Trans Fat), Cholesterol (Chol), Sodium (Sod), Carbohydrates (Carb), Dietary Fiber (Fib), Protein (Prot), and Calcium (Calc).

- Nutritional information for recipes that include meat, poultry, and fish are based on cooked skinless boneless portions (unless otherwise stated), with the fat trimmed.

- We recommend that you buy lean meat and poultry, then trim it of all visible fat before cooking. When poultry is cooked with the skin on, we suggest removing the skin before eating.

- Before serving, divide foods—including any vegetables, sauce, or accompaniments—into portions of equal size according to the designated number of servings per recipe.

- Any substitutions made to the ingredients will alter the "Per serving" nutritional information and may affect the **Core Plan** recipe status or the *POINTS* value.

- It is implied that all fresh fruits, vegetables, and greens in recipes should be rinsed before using.

Contents

Appetizers, Light Bites, and Soups

☑ Grill-Roasted Eggplant Dip

Delicate leaves of Belgian endive, topped with this chunky eggplant dip, make an elegant starter for a late summer barbecue. This dip also goes beautifully with raw vegetables, such as colorful strips of bell peppers, zucchini, or summer squash.

MAKES 4 SERVINGS 🥕

- 1 (1-pound) eggplant
- 2 tablespoons minced fresh parsley
- 2 tablespoons fresh lemon juice
- 1 tablespoon minced onion
- 1 garlic clove
- ¼ teaspoon salt
- ⅛ teaspoon freshly ground pepper
- 2 large Belgian endives, leaves separated

Spray the grill rack with nonstick spray; prepare the grill for a medium fire using the direct method (see page 81).

Slice the eggplant in half lengthwise; gently cut a ½-inch cross hatch pattern through the flesh with a paring knife, being careful not to pierce the skin.

Place the eggplant halves skin-side down on the coolest part of the grill and grill for 25 minutes, until the pulp is soft. Allow them to cool slightly, then scoop the pulp from the shells, avoiding any burned parts. Discard the shells.

Combine the grilled eggplant, parsley, lemon juice, onion, garlic, salt, and pepper in a blender or food processor; puree until blended to the consistency of lumpy oatmeal.

Transfer the dip to a small serving bowl; cover and refrigerate if you are not serving at once. Place the bowl on a platter and surround with the endive leaves.

PER SERVING (¼ cup dip with 5 endive leaves): 50 Cal, 0 g Fat, 0 g Sat Fat, 0 g Trans Fat, 0 mg Chol, 137 mg Sod, 12 g Carb, 4 g Fib, 2 g Prot, 57 mg Calc. *POINTS* value: *0.*

FROM RIGHT, CLOCKWISE: GRILLED PITA
WEDGES WITH INDIAN YOGURT DIP (PAGE 13),
BEAN AND ZUCCHINI DIP (PAGE 12) WITH
GRILLED BAGEL CHIPS (PAGE 21), AND
GRILL-ROASTED EGGPLANT DIP (OPPOSITE)

Bean and Zucchini Dip

A platter of fresh crudités absolutely sparkles when accompanied by this Italian-style dip. Or, serve with Grilled Bagel Chips (page 21) and deduct them from your **weekly** *POINTS* **Allowance.**

MAKES 8 SERVINGS

1 **medium zucchini, thinly sliced lengthwise**	1–2 **tablespoons fresh lemon juice**
2 **cups drained, rinsed cannellini (white kidney) beans**	1–2 **garlic cloves, minced**
	2 **teaspoons olive oil**
2 **tablespoons minced fresh parsley**	½ **teaspoon salt**
	¼ **teaspoon freshly ground pepper**

Spray the grill rack with nonstick spray; prepare the grill for a medium fire using the direct method (see page 81).

Place the zucchini slices on the grill rack, and grill, turning once, until lightly charred and fork-tender, about 5 minutes.

Combine the zucchini, beans, parsley, lemon juice, garlic, oil, salt, and pepper in a blender or food processor; puree.

Transfer to a serving bowl, or cover and refrigerate for up to 2 days if not serving at once.

PER SERVING (¼ cup): 64 Cal, 2 g Fat, 0 g Sat Fat, 0 g Trans Fat, 0 mg Chol, 88 mg Sod, 0 g Carb, 3 g Fib, 4 g Prot, 21 mg Calc. *POINTS* value: *1.*

Grilled Pita Wedges with Indian Yogurt Dip

This refreshing yogurt-based condiment, known as raita (pronounced RAY-ta) in India, is served with toasted pita wedges, and makes a delicious starter for a light summer barbecue.

MAKES 4 SERVINGS

½ teaspoon cumin seeds

2 cups plain fat-free yogurt

2 medium cucumbers, pared, halved, seeded, and grated

¼ cup finely minced red onion

1 tablespoon + 1 teaspoon minced fresh mint

½ teaspoon salt

2 (6-inch) pita breads, halved horizontally

Toast the cumin seeds in a small skillet over low heat until just fragrant, about 2 minutes. Transfer the seeds to a cutting board and crush them with a mallet or the flat side of a large knife, or crush with a mortar and pestle.

Combine the yogurt, cucumbers, onion, mint, salt, and crushed cumin in a small bowl. Cover and refrigerate for about 1 hour.

Spray the grill rack with nonstick spray; prepare the grill for a medium fire using the direct method (see page 81).

Place the pita halves on the grill rack, and grill until golden and crisp, being careful not to let them burn, 1–2 minutes on each side. Cut each pita half into 8 wedges, making a total of 32 wedges.

Place the bowl of raita on a platter, surround with the toasted pita wedges, and serve at once.

PER SERVING (½ cup raita with 8 pita wedges): 153 Cal, 1 g Fat, 0 g Sat Fat, 0 g Trans Fat, 2 mg Chol, 516 mg Sod, 27 g Carb, 1 g Fib, 10 g Prot, 266 mg Calc. *POINTS* value: *3.*

TIP If you prefer, you can toast the pitas in a conventional oven or toaster.

Vegetable Kebabs with Yogurt Sauce

Piping hot grilled vegetables are balanced with a refreshing lemon-yogurt sauce in this delightful Mediterranean appetizer. The kebabs are also delicious served cold or at room temperature as a salad.

MAKES 4 SERVINGS

5 scallions, chopped

½ cup plain fat-free yogurt

½ teaspoon grated lemon zest

2 tablespoons fresh lemon juice

1 teaspoon hot pepper sauce

¼ teaspoon salt

⅛ teaspoon freshly ground pepper

1 medium zucchini, halved lengthwise and cut into 1-inch chunks

1 medium yellow squash, halved lengthwise and cut into 1-inch chunks

6 ounces fresh white mushrooms, quartered

18 cherry tomatoes

2 teaspoons olive oil

Spray the grill rack with nonstick spray; prepare the grill for a medium fire using the direct method (see page 81). If using wooden skewers, soak them first in water for 30 minutes.

To make the yogurt sauce, combine the scallions, yogurt, lemon zest, lemon juice, pepper sauce, salt, and pepper in a small bowl; set aside.

Thread the zucchini, squash, mushrooms, and tomatoes onto 8 (12-inch) metal or wooden skewers, dividing evenly and alternating to create a colorful pattern; brush the vegetables with the oil.

Place the kebabs on the grill rack, and grill, turning once, until the vegetables are lightly charred and softened, about 10 minutes. Place 2 kebabs on each of 4 plates; serve with the sauce.

PER SERVING (2 kebabs with 3 tablespoons sauce): 74 Cal, 3 g Fat, 0 g Sat Fat, 0 g Trans Fat, 1 mg Chol, 199 mg Sod, 10 g Carb, 2 g Fib, 4 g Prot, 86 mg Calc. *POINTS* value: *1.*

 Fresh Tomato Salsa

You might like to serve this classic salsa as a delightful accompaniment to grilled meat, chicken, or fish. Or, serve it as an appetizer with crudités or baked tortilla chips. Remember to deduct the chips from your **weekly *POINTS* Allowance.**

MAKES 4 SERVINGS

1½ **cups seeded, diced ripe tomatoes**

1 **onion, diced**

2 **tablespoons minced fresh cilantro**

1 **tablespoon minced jalapeño pepper (wear gloves to prevent irritation)**

2 **teaspoons balsamic vinegar**

2 **garlic cloves, minced**

¼ **teaspoon salt**

Combine the tomatoes, onion, cilantro, jalapeño, vinegar, garlic, and salt in a medium bowl; stir well. Cover and set aside at least 1 hour to blend the flavors. Or, refrigerate, covered, for up to 1 day.

PER SERVING (½ cup): 28 Cal, 0 g Fat, 0 g Sat Fat, 0 g Trans Fat, 0 mg Chol, 143 mg Sod, 6 g Carb, 1 g Fib, 1 g Prot, 13 mg Calc. *POINTS* value: **0.**

TIP Be sure to use the ripest, juiciest tomatoes for the best flavor.

GRILLED TROPICAL SALSA

Grilled Tropical Salsa

This sweet-and-sour pineapple salsa complements grilled fish and chicken very well.

MAKES 4 SERVINGS

- ¾ cup diced Maple-Glazed Pineapple (page 218)
- 3 tablespoons coarsely chopped red onion
- ½ teaspoon chili powder
- 1 garlic clove, finely minced
- ⅛ teaspoon salt
- Pinch cayenne or dash hot pepper sauce
- 1 tablespoon chopped fresh cilantro
- ½ teaspoon cider vinegar

Combine the pineapple, onion, chili powder, garlic, salt, and cayenne in a bowl. Add the cilantro and vinegar. If the pineapple is very sweet, add more vinegar to taste. Serve at once, or cover and refrigerate until ready to use, up to 3 days.

PER SERVING (¼ cup): 39 Cal, 0 g Fat, 0 g Sat Fat, 0 g Trans Fat, 0 mg Chol, 24 mg Sod, 10 g Carb, 1 g Fib, 0 g Prot, 12 mg Calc. *POINTS* value: *1.*

CHOOSING A GRILL

Charcoal Grills Purists tend to like charcoal grills because you get that great barbecue taste. Simple models include the traditional hibachi or brazier type, best for quick, direct cooking of burgers, steaks, chops, and kebabs. Covered grills such as the kettle barbecue, with a clamshell-shaped lid, or a box-shaped grill with a hinged lid are also popular.

Gas Grills For those who like convenience, the gas grill is the way to go—it can be ready in as little as 10 minutes. Gas grills have covers that allow for both open and closed grilling. They are fueled either by a refillable propane gas unit or through a permanent connection to a natural gas line.

Indoor Grills You can buy small electric units (some with built-in rotisseries) or a cast-iron grill pan with a raised-ridge surface, which sits directly on top of the stove.

Conventional Oven Broiler If you prefer, you can broil many of the recipes in this book. Simply spray the broiler rack with nonstick spray, and preheat the broiler. Broil the food, 4 to 5 inches from the heat, as directed in the grilled version.

Mushroom Bruschetta

This earthy dish makes a flavorsome appetizer for a meal of grilled vegetables, or a fine side dish with grilled poultry or beef. If you are using shiitake mushrooms, be sure to use a grill basket so that you don't lose any in the coals. Spray the basket with nonstick spray before using.

MAKES 4 SERVINGS

4 (½-inch-thick) slices Tuscan or peasant bread, 3½ × 6 inches

1 large garlic clove, halved

4 Portobello or 12 shiitake mushrooms (about ½ pound), stems removed

2 teaspoons olive oil

¼ cup minced shallots

¼ cup reduced-sodium chicken broth

1 tablespoon balsamic vinegar

Freshly ground pepper, to taste

Spray the grill rack with nonstick spray; prepare the grill for a medium fire using the direct method (see page 81).

Place the bread slices on the edges of the grill; toast just long enough to crisp and char them lightly. Turn with tongs, and toast the other sides.

Rub the bread with the garlic halves; wrap loosely in foil to keep warm.

Place the mushrooms on the edges of the grill, and grill just long enough to char them lightly. Wrap them in foil to steam and keep warm.

Heat the oil in a small skillet over medium heat or at the edge of the grill. Add the shallots and cook, stirring constantly, just until wilted, about 2 minutes. Add the broth, vinegar, and pepper; bring to a boil. Reduce the heat and simmer, uncovered, for 1 minute. Stir in the mushroom juices that have accumulated in the foil.

Slice the mushrooms and arrange them on the bread slices. Drizzle the oil mixture evenly over the mushrooms and serve at once.

PER SERVING (1 slice): 127 Cal, 3 g Fat, 1 g Sat Fat, 0 g Trans Fat, 0 mg Chol, 210 mg Sod, 20 g Carb, 2 g Fib, 4 g Prot, 33 mg Calc. *POINTS* value: *2.*

TIP This recipe also works very well with white or cremini mushrooms.

Fresh Tomato-Basil Bruschetta

For the best flavor, use juicy, ripe tomatoes and fresh basil. Avoid using dried basil—the flavor just isn't the same. If you like, you can substitute fresh mint or oregano for the basil.

MAKES 4 SERVINGS ⏲ 🥕

- 4 (½-inch-thick) slices Tuscan or peasant bread, 3½ × 6 inches
- 1 garlic clove, halved
- 8 fresh basil leaves, slivered
- 2 teaspoons olive oil
- 2 large ripe tomatoes, each cut into 8 slices

Spray the grill rack with nonstick spray; prepare the grill for a medium fire using the direct method (see page 81).

Place the bread slices on the edges of the grill rack; toast just long enough to crisp and char them lightly. Turn with tongs, and toast the other sides.

Rub the bread with the garlic halves; wrap loosely in foil to keep warm.

Combine the basil and oil in a small bowl, and gently toss the tomatoes in the mixture. Arrange the tomato slices on the bread slices and serve at once.

PER SERVING (1 slice): 117 Cal, 4 g Fat, 1 g Sat Fat, 0 g Trans Fat, 0 mg Chol, 174 mg Sod, 19 g Carb, 2 g Fib, 3 g Prot, 29 mg Calc. *POINTS* value: *2.*

Two-Cheese Bread

Here's garlic bread and more. Mozzarella and Parmesan cheeses plus fresh basil make this a decadently rich bread that's great for company, and kids will love it too. If you are a garlic fan, use 3 or 4 garlic cloves.

MAKES 4 SERVINGS 🕒 🥕

⅓ cup shredded part-skim mozzarella cheese

1½ tablespoons freshly grated Parmesan cheese

½ cup minced fresh basil

2 garlic gloves, minced

¼ teaspoon freshly ground pepper

1 small loaf French bread (about 4 ounces), halved horizontally

Prepare the grill for a medium fire using the direct method (see page 81).

Combine the mozzarella and Parmesan cheeses, basil, garlic, and pepper in a small bowl; toss well. Sprinkle the cheese mixture over the cut sides of the bread; press firmly onto the bread with your fingers. Put the bread together, sandwich-style; wrap the loaf in heavy-duty foil.

Place the loaf on the grill rack and grill, turning once, until it is hot and the cheese is melted, 8–10 minutes. Remove the foil and cut the bread into 8 slices. Serve at once.

PER SERVING (2 slices): 122 Cal, 3 g Fat, 2 g Sat Fat, 1 g Trans Fat, 7 mg Chol, 267 mg Sod, 18 g Carb, 1 g Fib, 6 g Prot, 123 mg Calc. *POINTS* value: *2.*

Grilled Bagel Chips

Flavor these versatile chips with any combination of dried herbs and spices. They go especially well with Bean and Zucchini Dip (page 12).

MAKES 4 SERVINGS ○ ✈

1 (4-ounce) bagel, halved horizontally then sliced into 16 pieces

1 teaspoon olive oil

Pinch salt

Pinch garlic powder

Pinch dried oregano

Spray the grill rack with nonstick spray; prepare the grill for a medium fire using the direct method (see page 81).

Place the bagel pieces on the grill rack and grill, turning once using tongs, until golden brown, 2–3 minutes.

Combine the oil, salt, garlic powder, and oregano on a shallow plate. Toss the chips in the oil and seasonings until well coated. Transfer to a serving bowl.

PER SERVING (4 chips): 88 Cal, 2 g Fat, 0 g Sat Fat, 0 g Trans Fat, 0 mg Chol, 184 mg Sod, 15 g Carb, 1 g Fib, 3 g Prot, 22 mg Calc. **POINTS** value: **2.**

TIP If you have a grill basket, spray it with nonstick spray and place the bagel pieces in it to help keep them from falling through the grill grates.

Creamy Corn Chowder

Smoky roasted corn gives extra flavor to this comforting classic soup. You might consider making it ahead—it's even better the next day.

MAKES 4 SERVINGS

- 2 teaspoons butter
- 1 medium yellow bell pepper, seeded and diced
- 1 medium onion, diced
- ½ cup diced celery
- ¼ cup minced shallots
- 2 tablespoons all-purpose flour
- 1 cup reduced-sodium chicken broth
- 1 large (10-ounce) potato, peeled and diced
- ½ teaspoon salt
- ¼ teaspoon ground white pepper
- ¼ teaspoon paprika
- 1 bay leaf
- 4 ears Grilled Corn on the Cob, kernels removed to give about 2 cups (see page 116)
- 2 cups low-fat (1%) milk
- ½ teaspoon hot pepper sauce
- 2 tablespoons minced fresh chives

Melt the butter in a large nonstick saucepan. Add the bell pepper, onion, celery, and shallots; cook, stirring constantly, until softened, about 10 minutes. Add the flour and cook, stirring constantly, until lightly browned, about 2 minutes. Stir in the broth, potato, salt, pepper, paprika, and bay leaf; bring to a boil. Reduce the heat and simmer, covered, about 20 minutes.

Add the corn, milk, and pepper sauce; return to a boil. Reduce the heat to very low and simmer 15 minutes more, but do not allow to boil.

Remove the soup from the heat and discard the bay leaf. Divide the soup evenly among 4 bowls; garnish each with 1½ teaspoons minced chives.

PER SERVING (1½ cups): 243 Cal, 5 g Fat, 2 g Sat Fat, 0 g Trans Fat, 10 mg Chol, 555 mg Sod, 45 g Carb, 5 g Fib, 10 g Prot, 175 mg Calc. **POINTS** value: **4.**

CREAMY CORN CHOWDER

Grilled Mushroom–Rice Soup

Grilled mushrooms give this soup a full, earthy flavor. It's a perfect starter for a roast turkey or beef main course, or it makes a light and delicious lunch or late supper. The recipe is easily doubled.

MAKES 4 SERVINGS

¼ cup balsamic vinegar

3 teaspoons olive oil

2 large (4-inch) Portobello mushrooms

½ pound fresh white mushrooms

1 small onion, chopped

2 garlic cloves, minced

4 cups water

3 tablespoons long-grain white rice

2 teaspoons minced fresh thyme, or ½ teaspoon dried

1 teaspoon reduced-sodium soy sauce

¼ cup minced fresh parsley

¼ teaspoon salt

¼ teaspoon freshly ground pepper

Prepare the grill for a low fire using the direct method (see page 81). Spray a grill basket with nonstick spray.

Combine the vinegar and 1 teaspoon of the oil in a medium bowl; add the Portobello and white mushrooms and toss well.

Place the mushrooms in the grill basket, and grill, turning once, until cooked through, 15–20 minutes.

Meanwhile, heat the remaining 2 teaspoons oil in a medium nonstick saucepan. Add the onion and cook, stirring frequently, until translucent, about 4 minutes. Add the garlic and cook, stirring, 1 minute more. Add the water, rice, thyme, and soy sauce; bring to a boil. Reduce the heat and simmer until the rice is cooked, about 15 minutes.

Combine the mushrooms and 1 cup of the rice mixture in a blender or food processor; puree. Return the puree to the saucepan with the remaining rice mixture; cook and stir until heated. Stir in the parsley, salt, and pepper.

PER SERVING (1 cup): 103 Cal, 4 g Fat, 1 g Sat Fat, 0 g Trans Fat, 0 mg Chol, 192 mg Sod, 15 g Carb, 2 g Fib, 3 g Prot, 23 mg Calc. *POINTS* value: *2.*

Chilled Borscht

When the beets are cooked on a grill, this traditional Russian beet soup picks up an entirely new flavor. If you buy beets in a bunch, trim the greens and use a few finely minced leaves to garnish the soup. Or, save the greens to add to other soups or to cook as you would spinach.

MAKES 4 SERVINGS

- 6 medium beets (about 1½ pounds), trimmed and rinsed
- 2 cups reduced-sodium chicken broth
- 1 cup shredded cabbage
- 1 cup cranberry juice cocktail
- ½ cup diced onion
- 1 tablespoon sugar
- ½ teaspoon salt
- ¼ cup fat-free sour cream

Spray the grill rack with nonstick spray; prepare the grill for a low fire using the direct method (see page 81).

Place the beets on the grill rack, and grill, turning occasionally, until tender, 35–45 minutes. Let the beets cool, then peel and dice them. There should be about 2 cups.

Combine the beets, broth, cabbage, cranberry juice, onion, sugar, and salt in a medium nonstick saucepan; bring to a boil. Reduce the heat and simmer, stirring frequently, about 40 minutes. Let the mixture cool about 30 minutes, then refrigerate, covered, 3–4 hours. Serve the soup with the sour cream.

PER SERVING (1 cup soup with 1 tablespoon sour cream): 149 Cal, 0 g Fat, 0 g Sat Fat, 0 g Trans Fat, 0 mg Chol, 755 mg Sod, 33 g Carb, 4 g Fib, 5 g Prot, 61 mg Calc.
POINTS value: **2.**

TIP This soup can also be served hot, with or without the sour cream.

Grilled Gazpacho

This classic chilled soup gets a delicious smoky twist by grilling the vegetables. Make a double batch and store the extra in the refrigerator in an airtight container for up to 2 days.

MAKES 4 SERVINGS

- 1 **large red onion, quartered**
- 1 **large green bell pepper, seeded and quartered**
- 8 **large plum tomatoes, halved**
- 3 **garlic cloves, chopped**
- 2 **tablespoons fresh lime juice**
- 1 **tablespoon balsamic or red-wine vinegar**

- ½ **teaspoon salt**
- ½ **teaspoon freshly ground pepper**
- **Hot pepper sauce, to taste**
- ½ **cup seeded and diced cucumber**

Spray the grill rack with nonstick spray; prepare the grill for a medium fire using the direct method (see page 81).

Place the onion and bell pepper on the grill rack, and grill, turning once, until slightly charred on all sides, 8–10 minutes. After 7–8 minutes, add the tomatoes to the grill rack, and grill for 2–3 minutes.

Puree the grilled onion, bell pepper, and tomatoes with the garlic, lime juice, vinegar, salt, and pepper in a blender or food processor until smooth. Season to taste with the pepper sauce. Transfer to a bowl, cover, and refrigerate until chilled, at least 2 hours or up to overnight. Serve topped with the cucumber.

PER SERVING (1 cup soup with 2 tablespoons diced cucumber): 62 Cal, 1 g Fat, 0 g Sat Fat, 0 g Trans Fat, 0 mg Chol, 291 mg Sod, 14 g Carb, 3 g Fib, 2 g Prot, 32 mg Calc. **POINTS** value: *1.*

Chilled Fruit Soup with Mint

This refreshing soup is a great way to start—or finish—a meal on a hot summer evening. If you like, substitute an equal amount of nectarines for the peaches.

MAKES 4 SERVINGS

4 fresh peaches, peeled, pitted, and quartered

2 cups diced cantaloupe

1 cup fresh orange juice

3 tablespoons fresh lemon juice

1 tablespoon minced fresh mint

4 whole mint leaves

Spray the grill rack with nonstick spray; prepare the grill for a medium-hot fire using the direct method (see page 81). Spray a grill basket with nonstick spray.

Place the peaches in the grill basket in a single layer and grill about 3 minutes on each side.

Combine the grilled peaches, the cantaloupe, orange juice, lemon juice, and minced mint in a blender or food processor; puree. Transfer the soup to a bowl, cover, and refrigerate until chilled, at least 3 hours or up to overnight. Serve the soup, garnished with the whole mint leaves.

PER SERVING (1¼ cups): 114 Cal, 0 g Fat, 0 g Sat Fat, 0 g Trans Fat, 0 mg Chol, 8 mg Sod, 28 g Carb, 3 g Fib, 2 g Prot, 23 mg Calc. **POINTS** value: **2.**

TIP To peel a peach, dip it in boiling water for about 30 seconds. Remove it with a slotted spoon, then gently peel the skin with a paring knife.

Sizzling Meats— Steaks, Chops, Burgers, and More

Herb and Mustard Beef Tenderloin

Thinly sliced, this elegant beef is wonderful for a special summer party. Take care not to overcook the meat. Serve with Minted Green Beans (page 130).

MAKES 4 SERVINGS

¼ cup minced fresh parsley

1 tablespoon minced fresh rosemary

1 teaspoon minced fresh thyme

4 garlic cloves, minced

1 tablespoon Dijon mustard

1 teaspoon olive oil

½ teaspoon freshly ground pepper

1 (1-pound) lean beef tenderloin

Combine the parsley, rosemary, thyme, garlic, mustard, oil, and pepper in a small bowl. Spread the mixture on the tenderloin, wrap in plastic wrap, and refrigerate for 30 minutes.

Spray the grill rack with nonstick spray; prepare the grill for a medium fire using the direct method (see page 81).

Remove and discard the plastic wrap. Place the tenderloin on the grill rack and grill, turning frequently, until an instant-read thermometer inserted in the center of the tenderloin registers 145°F for medium-rare, about 20 minutes, or 160°F for medium, about 22 minutes. Transfer the beef to a cutting board and let stand about 5 minutes. Cut into 16 slices.

PER SERVING (4 slices tenderloin): 166 Cal, 8 g Fat, 3 g Sat Fat, 1 g Trans Fat, 57 mg Chol, 141 mg Sod, 2 g Carb, 0 g Fib, 20 g Prot, 24 mg Calc. *POINTS* value: *4.*

HERB AND MUSTARD
BEEF TENDERLOIN

Argentine Brisket

The Argentine barbecue, where meats are fire-roasted in foil, serves as inspiration for this spicy beef dish served with a hot, tangy sauce that enhances its richness. Leftovers are delicious cold.

MAKES 24 SERVINGS

1 (4-pound) lean beef brisket
1 large onion, finely chopped
6 garlic cloves, finely minced
2 teaspoons coarsely ground
  black pepper

1 teaspoon sugar
½–2 teaspoons cayenne
1½ cups Jalapeño Green Sauce
  (page 200)

With a sharp knife, pierce the brisket at 2-inch intervals, making 1-inch-deep slits. Combine the onion, garlic, pepper, sugar, and cayenne in a small bowl. Pack the mixture into the slits, rubbing any extra over the meat. Wrap the brisket in a double layer of heavy-duty foil and refrigerate overnight.

Spray the grill rack with nonstick spray; prepare the grill for a low fire using the indirect method (see page 81).

Place the foil-wrapped brisket on the grill rack. Close the grill, with the bottom vent open and top vent half open, and grill for 2 hours. If you are using a charcoal grill, add 5 lighted briquettes to each side of the coals every hour.

Remove the foil-wrapped brisket from the grill with long sturdy tongs. Holding the packet over a bowl, drain any juices. Remove and discard the foil; return the meat to the grill rack. Baste the meat with the juices. Cover and continue grilling for 1 hour longer, basting twice. Transfer the meat to a carving board, cover loosely with foil, and let stand about 10 minutes. Slice the brisket thinly across the grain into 48 slices and serve with the Jalapeño Green Sauce.

PER SERVING (2 slices brisket and 1 tablespoon sauce): 148 Cal, 8 g Fat, 3 g Sat Fat, 0 g Trans Fat, 53 mg Chol, 423 mg Sod, 1 g Carb, 0 g Fib, 17 g Prot, 88 mg Calc.
POINTS value: *4.*

T-Bone Steak with Horseradish Sauce

This wickedly indulgent steak needs little embellishment to taste fantastic, so we
kept it simple—just a quick herb rub on the meat and a creamy horseradish sauce
for dipping. Try it with flank or top round steak too.

MAKES 4 SERVINGS

2 tablespoons fat-free
   sour cream
2 tablespoons fat-free
   mayonnaise
1 tablespoon prepared
   horseradish, squeezed dry
½ teaspoon dried oregano
½ teaspoon salt

¼ teaspoon dried thyme
¼ teaspoon fennel seeds,
   lightly crushed
¼ teaspoon freshly
   ground pepper
2 (¾-pound) lean T-bone steaks,
   about ½ inch thick

Spray the grill rack with nonstick spray; prepare the grill for a medium-hot fire
using the direct method (see page 81).

To make the sauce, combine the sour cream, mayonnaise, and horseradish
in a small bowl; mix well.

Combine the oregano, salt, thyme, fennel seeds, and pepper in a small bowl.
Rub the herb mixture over both sides of each steak.

Place the steaks on the grill rack and grill until an instant-read thermometer
inserted in the center of each steak registers 145°F for medium-rare,
4–4½ minutes on each side, or 160°F for medium, about 5 minutes on each
side. Transfer the steaks to a cutting board and let stand about 5 minutes.
Cut each steak in half and serve with the sauce.

PER SERVING (½ steak and about 1 tablespoon sauce): 174 Cal, 8 g Fat, 3 g Sat Fat,
1 g Trans Fat, 47 mg Chol, 429 mg Sod, 3 g Carb, 1 g Fib, 22 g Prot, 23 mg Calc.
POINTS value: *4.*

TIP To crush the fennel seeds, place the seeds in a zip-close plastic bag;
firmly tap the seeds with a meat mallet or the bottom of a heavy skillet.

Zesty London Broil

London broil is the popular name given to flank steak that has been marinated, then grilled or broiled, and thinly sliced on a diagonal. The piquant flavor of this marinade comes from the blending of three different types of vinegars.

MAKES 4 SERVINGS

½ cup finely chopped onion

¼ cup sherry vinegar

¼ cup red-wine vinegar

¼ cup dry red wine

2 tablespoons reduced-sodium soy sauce

1 tablespoon balsamic vinegar

6 garlic cloves, coarsely chopped

2 teaspoons olive oil

1 tablespoon sugar

1 teaspoon grated peeled fresh ginger or ½ teaspoon ground

Freshly ground pepper, to taste

1 (1-pound) lean flank steak

Combine the onion, sherry vinegar, red-wine vinegar, wine, soy sauce, balsamic vinegar, garlic, oil, sugar, ginger, and pepper in a zip-close plastic bag; add the steak. Squeeze out the air and seal the bag; turn to coat the meat. Refrigerate, turning the bag after 2 hours, for at least 4 hours or up to overnight. Remove the steak from the marinade.

Pour the marinade into a small saucepan and boil, stirring constantly, for 3 minutes. Remove the marinade from the heat and set aside.

Spray the grill rack with nonstick spray; prepare the grill for a hot fire using the direct method (see page 81).

Place the steak on the grill rack and grill the steak, basting with the marinade, until an instant-read thermometer inserted in the center of the steak registers 145°F for medium-rare, 7–9 minutes on each side, or 160°F for medium, 9–10 minutes on each side. Transfer the steak to a cutting board and let stand about 5 minutes. Cut the steak across the grain into 16 diagonal slices.

PER SERVING (4 slices steak): 228 Cal, 11 g Fat, 4 g Sat Fat, 1 g Trans Fat, 54 mg Chol, 372 mg Sod, 9 g Carb, 1 g Fib, 23 g Prot, 19 mg Calc. *POINTS* value: *5.*

Marinated Flank Steak with Cherry Tomato Salad

If you like to plan meals ahead for busy weeknights, marinating a steak is a great idea. This marinade is a flavorful combination of garlic, shallot, soy sauce, balsamic vinegar, and thyme. We cook the steak on a grill, but you can also use a ridged grill pan and enjoy this dish year round—the cooking times will remain the same.

MAKES 4 SERVINGS

- 3 garlic cloves, minced
- 1 medium shallot, chopped
- 2 tablespoons reduced-sodium soy sauce
- 2 tablespoons balsamic vinegar
- 2 teaspoons olive oil
- ½ teaspoon dried thyme
- 1 (1-pound) lean flank steak
- 1 pint cherry tomatoes, halved
- ½ small red onion, finely chopped
- ¼ teaspoon salt

Combine the garlic, shallot, soy sauce, 1 tablespoon of the vinegar, 1 teaspoon of the oil, and the thyme in a zip-close plastic bag; add the steak. Squeeze out the air and seal the bag; turn to coat the steak. Refrigerate, turning the bag occasionally, at least 2 hours or overnight.

Meanwhile, to make the salad, combine the remaining 1 tablespoon vinegar and 1 teaspoon oil, the tomatoes, onion, and salt in a medium bowl.

Spray the grill rack with nonstick spray; prepare the grill for a medium-hot fire using the direct method (see page 81).

Remove the steak from the marinade; discard the marinade. Place the steak on the grill rack and grill until an instant-read thermometer inserted in the center of the steak registers 145°F for medium-rare, about 7 minutes on each side, or 160°F for medium, about 8 minutes on each side. Transfer the steak to a cutting board and let stand about 5 minutes. Cut the steak across the grain into 16 diagonal slices and serve with the tomato salad.

PER SERVING (4 steak slices with ½ cup salad): 202 Cal, 11 g Fat, 4 g Sat Fat, 1 g Trans Fat, 48 mg Chol, 278 mg Sod, 6 g Carb, 1 g Fib, 20 g Prot, 12 mg Calc. *POINTS* value: *5.*

TIP This recipe also works beautifully with lean top round steak.

GRILLED MUSTARD-
CRUMBED FLANK STEAK
WITH VEGETABLES

Grilled Mustard-Crumbed Flank Steak with Vegetables

This steak with vegetables is full of rich, spicy flavor. Serve with leafy greens and a crusty roll to complete the meal. Any leftover steak is delicious the next day layered with thinly sliced red onion in a hearty sandwich.

MAKES 4 SERVINGS

- 1 tablespoon plain dry bread crumbs
- 1 tablespoon canola oil
- 1 tablespoon minced scallion
- 1 tablespoon coarse-grained mustard

- 1 teaspoon Worcestershire sauce
- 2 cups seeded and sliced green bell peppers
- 2 medium tomatoes, cut into ½-inch-thick slices
- 1 (1-pound) lean flank steak

Spray the grill rack with nonstick spray; prepare the grill for a medium fire using the direct method (see page 81). Spray a grill basket with nonstick spray.

Combine the bread crumbs, oil, scallion, mustard, and Worcestershire sauce in a small bowl; set aside.

Arrange the bell peppers and tomatoes in the grill basket. Place the steak and the grill basket on the grill rack and grill the steak and the vegetables 5 minutes. Transfer the tomatoes to a plate and keep warm. Turn the steak and the bell peppers. Spread the top of the steak with the crumb mixture. Grill until an instant-read thermometer inserted in the center of the steak registers 145°F for medium-rare, about 5 minutes longer, or 160°F for medium, about 6 minutes longer, and the bell peppers are tender, about 2 minutes. Transfer the steak to a cutting board and let stand about 5 minutes. Cut the steak across the grain into thin diagonal slices. Serve the steak with one-fourth of the vegetables.

PER SERVING (about 5 slices steak and ¼ of vegetables): 236 Cal, 12 g Fat, 4 g Sat Fat, 1 g Trans Fat, 54 mg Chol, 192 mg Sod, 7 g Carb, 2 g Fib, 23 g Prot, 19 mg Calc.
POINTS value: *5.*

Steak Roulade

Stuffed with raisins, parsley, and pine nuts, this roulade is not only delicious; it also makes a pretty presentation when sliced.

MAKES 4 SERVINGS

1 (1-pound) lean flank steak
¼ teaspoon salt
¼ teaspoon freshly ground pepper
1 garlic clove, minced
1 tablespoon raisins, chopped

1 tablespoon pine nuts, coarsely chopped
2 teaspoons coarsely chopped flat-leaf parsley

Spray the grill rack with nonstick spray; prepare the grill for a medium fire using the direct method (see page 81).

Sprinkle the steak with the salt and pepper. Evenly distribute the garlic, raisins, pine nuts, and parsley over one side of the steak. Starting at one short end, tightly roll up the steak jelly-roll fashion. Secure the meat lengthwise with a metal skewer; close the ends with toothpicks to keep the filling enclosed.

Place the roulade on the grill rack and grill, turning frequently, until browned and cooked through, 25–30 minutes. Transfer the roulade to a cutting board and let stand about 5 minutes. Remove the skewer and the toothpicks; carefully cut the roulade into 8 slices, keeping each slice intact.

PER SERVING (2 slices): 190 Cal, 9 g Fat, 4 g Sat Fat, 1 g Trans Fat, 54 mg Chol, 214 mg Sod, 3 g Carb, 0 g Fib, 23 g Prot, 10 mg Calc. *POINTS* value: *5.*

Barbecued Beef on a Bun

The sweet-and-vinegary tomato sauce, spooned over grilled steak slices, makes this very much like a Kansas City barbecue special. Some might say even better than Texas barbecue!

MAKES 6 SERVINGS

2 tablespoons red-wine vinegar
3 teaspoons canola oil
1 teaspoon paprika
1 garlic clove, minced
1 (1½-pound) lean flank steak
½ cup grated onion

¼ cup ketchup
2 teaspoons dark molasses
1 teaspoon chili powder
1 teaspoon steak sauce
6 (1-ounce) hard rolls, split

Combine the vinegar, 2 teaspoons of the oil, the paprika, and garlic in a zip-close plastic bag; add the steak. Squeeze out the air and seal the bag; turn to coat the steak. Refrigerate at least 6 hours or overnight. Transfer the steak to a platter and drizzle with any remaining marinade.

Spray the grill rack with nonstick spray; prepare the grill for a medium-hot fire using the direct method (see page 81).

To make the barbecue sauce, combine the onion, ketchup, molasses, chili powder, steak sauce, and the remaining 1 teaspoon oil in a small bowl. Set aside 2 tablespoons of the sauce and spread the rest onto both sides of steak.

Place the steak on the grill rack and grill until an instant-read thermometer inserted in the thickest part of the steak registers 145°F for medium-rare, about 4½ minutes on each side, or 160°F for medium, about 5 minutes on each side. Transfer the steak to a cutting board and let stand about 5 minutes. Cut the steak across the grain into 18 diagonal slices. Serve the steak slices in the hard rolls with the reserved barbecue sauce.

PER SERVING (3 slices steak on roll with 1 teaspoon sauce): 236 Cal, 9 g Fat, 3 g Sat Fat, 1 g Trans Fat, 36 mg Chol, 332 mg Sod, 20 g Carb, 1 g Fib, 18 g Prot, 40 mg Calc.
POINTS value: *5.*

Asian Beef Kebabs

A bed of shredded lettuce makes a typical accompaniment to these kebabs. Try adding a little grated carrot for color and texture.

MAKES 4 SERVINGS

- ¼ cup chopped scallions
- 2 tablespoons reduced-sodium soy sauce
- 1 tablespoon minced peeled fresh ginger
- 1 tablespoon rice-wine vinegar
- 2 teaspoons canola oil
- 1 teaspoon balsamic vinegar
- ½ teaspoon freshly ground pepper
- 1 garlic clove, minced
- ¾ pound lean beef tenderloin, cut into 16 strips
- ¼ cup Chinese mustard

Spray the grill rack with nonstick spray; prepare the grill for a hot fire (see page 81) using the direct method. If using wooden skewers, soak them in water for 30 minutes.

Combine the scallions, soy sauce, ginger, rice-wine vinegar, oil, balsamic vinegar, pepper, and garlic in a zip-close plastic bag; add the beef. Squeeze out the air and seal the bag; turn to coat the beef. Let stand for at least 15 minutes or refrigerate up to overnight.

Remove the beef from the marinade; discard any remaining marinade. On each of 16 (6-inch) metal or wooden skewers, thread 1 beef strip by piercing the beef in several places. Place the kebabs on the grill rack and grill 5 minutes. Turn the kebabs and grill until cooked through, about 5 minutes longer. Serve the kebabs with the mustard on the side.

PER SERVING (4 kebabs with 1 tablespoon mustard): 140 Cal, 7 g Fat, 3 g Sat Fat, 1 g Trans Fat, 42 mg Chol, 333 mg Sod, 3 g Carb, 0 g Fib, 14 g Prot, 5 mg Calc. *POINTS* value: *3.*

ASIAN BEEF KEBABS

Moroccan-Spiced Beef Kebabs

Sweet and aromatic, as opposed to fiery-hot, these simple kebabs with cumin, coriander, saffron, and cinnamon are equally wonderful as a family meal or for casual entertaining.

MAKES 4 SERVINGS

1 tablespoon extra-virgin olive oil

1 tablespoon fresh lemon juice

2 teaspoons grated lemon zest

1 teaspoon grated orange zest

1 teaspoon ground cumin

1/2 teaspoon ground coriander

1/2 teaspoon sugar

1/4 teaspoon ground saffron

1/4 teaspoon freshly ground pepper

1/8 teaspoon cinnamon

3/4 pound lean beef tenderloin, cut into 1-inch cubes

1 zucchini, halved lengthwise and cut crosswise into 16 pieces

1 teaspoon salt

Lemon wedges

Combine the oil, lemon juice, lemon zest, orange zest, cumin, coriander, sweetener, saffron, pepper and cinnamon in a zip-close plastic bag; add the beef. Squeeze out the air and seal the bag; turn to coat the beef. Refrigerate, turning the bag occasionally, at least 2 hours or overnight.

Spray the grill rack with nonstick spray; prepare the grill for a medium-hot fire using the direct method (see page 81). If using wooden skewers, soak them in water for 30 minutes.

Alternately thread the beef and zucchini onto 4 (10-inch) metal or wooden skewers. Sprinkle the kebabs with the salt and place on the grill rack. Grill the kebabs, turning every 2 minutes, until the beef is cooked as desired, 8–10 minutes for medium-rare. Serve with lemon wedges.

PER SERVING (1 kebab): 160 Cal, 10 g Fat, 3 g Sat Fat, 1 g Trans Fat, 42 mg Chol, 616 mg Sod, 3 g Carb, 1 g Fib, 15 g Prot, 21 mg Calc. *POINTS* value: **4.**

Jerk Beef Kebabs

Get in on the secret—super-tender beef tenderloin is a wonderful cut to use for kebabs. We thread the beef with sweet red bell peppers and ripe mango, which offer the perfect balance to the fiery jerk marinade.

MAKES 4 SERVINGS

- 3 scallions, chopped
- ¼ cup chopped fresh cilantro
- 2 garlic cloves, peeled
- 1 jalapeño pepper
- 2 tablespoons white vinegar
- 2 tablespoons reduced-sodium soy sauce
- 1 teaspoon ground allspice

- ¼ teaspoon cinnamon
- ¾ pound beef tenderloin, cut into 16 (¾-inch) cubes
- 1 red bell pepper, seeded and cut into 16 pieces
- 1 mango, peeled and cut into 16 cubes
- ¼ teaspoon salt

Combine the scallions, cilantro, garlic, jalapeño, vinegar, soy sauce, allspice, and cinnamon in a blender; process to form a paste. Transfer the paste to a zip-close plastic bag; add the beef. Squeeze out the air and seal the bag; turn to coat the beef. Refrigerate, turning the bag occasionally, at least 4 hours or up to overnight.

Spray the grill rack with nonstick spray; prepare the grill for a medium-hot fire using the direct method (see page 81).

Alternately thread 4 pieces of the beef, bell pepper, and mango onto 4 (12-inch) metal skewers. Sprinkle the kebabs with the salt and place on the grill rack. Grill the kebabs, turning every 2 minutes, until the beef is cooked as desired, about 8 minutes for medium-rare.

PER SERVING (1 kebab): 163 Cal, 5 g Fat, 2 g Sat Fat, 1 g Trans Fat, 43 mg Chol, 484 mg Sod, 13 g Carb, 2 g Fib, 16 g Prot, 27 mg Calc. **POINTS** value: **3.**

TIP To cut the mango into cubes, with a sharp knife, cut a lengthwise slice from each side of the long flat seed, as close to the seed as possible. Peel the seed section. Cut off as much flesh as possible; discard the seed. Cut the mango pieces lengthwise into thick wedges. Remove the peel from each wedge, cutting close to the peel. Cut each wedge into cubes.

HERBED BEEF BURGERS

Herbed Beef Burgers

A slice of juicy tomato and a crisp lettuce leaf is all you need to top this burger version of Italian meatballs.

MAKES 4 SERVINGS

2 (1-ounce) slices
  whole-wheat bread
1 pound ground lean beef
  (7% or less fat)
⅓ cup minced flat-leaf parsley
2 tablespoons freshly grated
  Parmesan cheese

3 garlic cloves, minced
1 teaspoon dried basil
½ teaspoon freshly
  ground pepper
¼ teaspoon salt
4 (1-ounce) hard rolls, split

Spray the grill rack with nonstick spray; prepare the grill for a medium fire using the direct method (see page 81).

Place the bread in a blender or food processor and pulse to a fine crumb.

Combine the beef, bread crumbs, parsley, cheese, garlic, basil, pepper, and salt in a large bowl. Shape the mixture into 4 equal patties.

Place the patties on the grill rack and grill until an instant-read thermometer inserted in the side of each patty registers 160°F for medium, about 5 minutes on each side. Serve each burger in a hard roll.

PER SERVING (1 burger in roll): 281 Cal, 8 g Fat, 3 g Sat Fat, 1 g Trans Fat, 67 mg Chol, 479 mg Sod, 23 g Carb, 2 g Fib, 28 g Prot, 97 mg Calc. *POINTS* value: *6.*

TIP Keep your hands and arms free from burns by using long-handled tools and long oven mitts when grilling.

Veal Chops with Honey-Mustard Glaze

Veal chops make an elegant entrée for any occasion, any season of the year. Try serving them with Baby Artichokes with Garlic and Lemon (page 125).

MAKES 4 SERVINGS

¼ cup balsamic vinegar

3 tablespoons fresh lemon juice

1 tablespoon Worcestershire sauce

2 teaspoons Dijon mustard

2 teaspoons honey

4 (3-ounce) veal loin chops

½ teaspoon salt

¼ teaspoon freshly ground pepper

Spray the grill rack with nonstick spray; prepare the grill for a hot fire using the direct method (see page 81).

To make the glaze, combine the vinegar, lemon juice, Worcestershire sauce, mustard, and honey in a small bowl.

Sprinkle the chops with the salt and pepper, then brush them with the glaze. Place the chops on the grill rack and grill, brushing them with the remaining glaze, until an instant-read thermometer inserted in the thickest part of the chops registers 145°F for medium-rare, about 2½ minutes on each side; or 160°F for medium, about 3 minutes on each side.

PER SERVING (1 veal chop): 121 Cal, 4 g Fat, 1 g Sat Fat, 1 g Trans Fat, 60 mg Chol, 433 mg Sod, 5 g Carb, 0 g Fib, 15 g Prot, 16 mg Calc. **POINTS** value: **3.**

GETTING THE GRILL READY

FOR CHARCOAL GRILLS: Pile the coals in the center of the barbecue; use starter fluid or an electric or chimney starter and light. The coals are ready when they are covered with a gray or white ash, in about 40 to 45 minutes. Place the rack on the grill's medium level, 4 to 5 inches from the coals.

FOR GAS GRILLS: Follow the manufacturer's instructions for lighting and preheating the grill.

MAINTAINING THE FIRE

FOR CHARCOAL GRILLS: You can raise or lower the grill rack—higher for longer, slower cooking, and lower for quicker, hotter cooking. Opening the side vents and letting in more air will cause the coals to burn faster and get hotter, closing them halfway will slow the fire, and closing them completely will extinguish it. Once the coals have been heated, here's how you get the temperature you want:

- **Low Fire** Spread out the coals, leaving ½-inch space between them, removing some coals if necessary. Close the vents halfway.
- **Medium Fire** Spread out the coals in a double layer so that they are still touching.
- **Hot Fire** Tap the ashes off the hot coals with tongs and move the coals closer together. Add a few more coals to fill (but do not use starter fluid). Open the vents fully.

FOR GAS GRILLS: Use the temperature control knobs to set the temperature indicated in the recipe. We specify the temperature (low, medium, or hot) to be used in every recipe in this book.

Grilled Pork Kebabs

The flavors of northern Italy—rosemary, sage, and garlic—are as delicious with pork as they are with chicken. If you substitute skinless boneless chicken breast for the pork in this recipe, marinate the chicken for only 30 minutes. Grilled tomatoes and a tossed green salad make very easy accompaniments.

MAKES 4 SERVINGS

½ cup dry white wine

2 teaspoons canola oil

1 teaspoon dried rosemary, crumbled

1 large garlic clove, minced

½ teaspoon dried sage, crumbled

⅛ teaspoon salt

⅛ teaspoon freshly ground pepper

¾ pound pork tenderloin, cut into 24 (¾-inch) pieces

2 cups cooked white rice

Spray the grill rack with nonstick spray; prepare the grill for a medium fire using the direct method (see page 81).

To make the marinade, combine the wine, oil, rosemary, garlic, sage, salt, and pepper in a zip-close plastic bag; add the pork. Squeeze out the air and seal the bag; turn to coat the pork. Refrigerate for 1 hour, turning the bag after 30 minutes. Remove the pork from the marinade. Discard the marinade.

Thread 3 pieces of pork onto each of 8 (12-inch) metal or wooden skewers. (If you are using wooden skewers, soak them in water for about 30 minutes before grilling.)

Place the kebabs on the grill rack and grill, turning occasionally, until cooked through, 5–7 minutes. Serve the kebabs with the rice.

PER SERVING (2 kebabs and ½ cup rice): 212 Cal, 4 g Fat, 1 g Sat Fat, 0 g Trans Fat, 47 mg Chol, 53 mg Sod, 22 g Carb, 1 g Fib, 19 g Prot, 14 mg Calc. *POINTS* value: *4.*

Pork Souvlaki with Cucumber-Yogurt Sauce

Traditional Greek souvlaki consists of lamb, marinated in lemon juice, olive oil, garlic, and oregano, then skewered. Here, we use lean pork tenderloin, with equally delicious results. We serve these kebabs with a creamy cucumber-yogurt sauce, but you can also make souvlaki sandwiches with chopped tomatoes, shredded romaine lettuce, and red onion on whole-wheat pita breads. Remember to deduct the pita from your **weekly *POINTS* Allowance.**

MAKES 4 SERVINGS

- 3 garlic cloves
- 2 tablespoons fresh lemon juice
- 2 teaspoons extra-virgin olive oil
- 1 teaspoon dried oregano
- 1 (1-pound) pork tenderloin, cut into 24 (1½-inch) cubes

- ½ medium cucumber, peeled and seeded
- ½ clup fat-free plain yogurt
- 2 teaspoons chopped fresh dill
- ½ teaspoon salt
- ¼ teaspoon freshly ground pepper

Mince 2 of the garlic cloves. Combine the minced garlic, the lemon juice, oil, and oregano in a zip-close plastic bag; add the pork. Squeeze out the air and seal the bag; turn to coat the pork. Refrigerate, turning the bag occasionally, at least 2 hours or overnight.

To make the yogurt sauce, mince the remaining garlic clove. Grate the cucumber; squeeze dry with a paper towel. Combine the garlic, cucumber, yogurt, and dill in a small bowl; mix well.

Spray the grill rack with olive oil nonstick spray; prepare the grill for a medium-hot fire using the direct method (see page 81).

Remove the pork from the marinade; discard the marinade. Thread 6 pieces of the pork onto each of 4 (10-inch) metal skewers. Sprinkle the kebabs with the salt and pepper. Place the kebabs on the grill rack and grill, turning every 2 minutes, until the pork is just cooked through, about 8 minutes. Serve the kebabs with the yogurt sauce.

PER SERVING (1 kebab and about 2½ tablespoons sauce): 156 Cal, 5 g Fat, 1 g Sat Fat, 0 g Trans Fat, 64 mg Chol, 353 mg Sod, 4 g Carb, 0 g Fib, 24 g Prot, 50 mg Calc. *POINTS* value: **4.**

TIP If you prefer the classic souvlaki, substitute chunks of lean boneless leg of lamb for the pork, or try chunks of skinless boneless chicken breasts.

Pork Cutlets with Apple-Onion Topping

This fruity dish makes a beautiful and fragrant autumn supper, especially when coupled with Grilled Sweet Potatoes with Lime (page 144). You can serve the apple mixture warm or make it ahead and serve it cold.

MAKES 4 SERVINGS

- **4 (¼-pound) boneless pork cutlets, trimmed**
- **½ teaspoon salt**
- **½ teaspoon freshly ground pepper**
- **½ teaspoon onion powder**
- **3 tablespoons Dijon mustard**

- **2 teaspoons canola oil**
- **1 onion, sliced into rings ¼-inch thick**
- **½ cup apple juice**
- **1 small Granny Smith apple, peeled, cored, and cut into ¼-inch-thick slices**

Spray the grill rack with nonstick spray; prepare the grill for a medium-hot fire using the direct method (see page 81).

Sprinkle both sides of the pork cutlets evenly with the salt, pepper, and onion powder; brush both sides evenly with the mustard and set aside.

To make the apple topping, heat the oil in a medium nonstick skillet over medium-high heat. Add the onion rings and cook, stirring frequently, until golden, about 10 minutes. Add the apple juice and simmer, 3 minutes. Add the apple slices and cook 5 minutes longer. Remove from the heat and keep warm.

Place the cutlets on the grill rack and grill until they are cooked through, about 6 minutes on each side. Serve the cutlets with the topping.

PER SERVING (1 cutlet with ¼ of topping): 242 Cal, 11 g Fat, 4 g Sat Fat, 0 g Trans Fat, 80 mg Chol, 493 mg Sod, 10 g Carb, 1 g Fib, 25 g Prot, 27 mg Calc. *POINTS* value: *6.*

**PORK CUTLETS WITH
APPLE-ONION TOPPPING**

Indian-Spiced Pork Chops

Yogurt, honey, and sweet spices give a delicate, delicious flavor to these pork chops.

MAKES 4 SERVINGS

2 tablespoons plain
   fat-free yogurt

2 teaspoons honey

2 garlic cloves, minced

1 teaspoon white-wine vinegar

½ teaspoon ground cumin

½ teaspoon ground ginger

¼ teaspoon ground turmeric

¼ teaspoon salt

⅛ teaspoon ground cloves

⅛ teaspoon cinnamon

⅛ teaspoon cayenne

4 (5-ounce) lean pork loin chops

Combine the yogurt, honey, garlic, vinegar, cumin, ginger, turmeric, salt, cloves, cinnamon, and cayenne in a zip-close plastic bag; add the pork. Squeeze out the air and seal the bag; turn to coat the pork. Refrigerate at least 2 hours or up to overnight.

Spray the grill rack with nonstick spray; prepare the grill for a medium fire using the direct method (see page 81).

Remove the chops from the marinade; discard the marinade. Place the chops on the grill rack and grill, turning once, until an instant-read thermometer inserted in the chop registers 160°F, about 4 minutes on each side.

PER SERVING (1 pork chop): 190 Cal, 7 g Fat, 3 g Sat Fat, 0 g Trans Fat, 70 mg Chol, 192 mg Sod, 4 g Carb, 0 g Fib, 26 g Prot, 47 mg Calc. **POINTS** value: **4.**

FEEL THE HEAT

Some grills come with temperature gauges, and you can find surface thermometers in hardware stores, but there's an easy way to gauge temperature with your hand. Simply place your hand, palm-side-down, 8 inches directly above the hot coals. Keep your hand there until the heat just starts to feel uncomfortable, counting the seconds. The fire will be:

low if you have to move your hand in 5 seconds

medium if you have to move your hand in 3 to 4 seconds

high if you have to move your hand in 2 seconds

 # Tandoori Lamb

Tandoori is one of the most famous dishes of India. It is named after the oven, a tandoor, in which it is traditionally prepared, but we use the grill in this recipe. The yogurt marinade helps tenderize the meat and imparts a tangy flavor, which allows the lamb to stand up to the intensely fragrant spices. If butterflied lamb is not available in the meat case at the supermarket, ask the butcher to prepare one for you, and when you get it home, be sure to trim it of all visible fat.

MAKES 8 SERVINGS

1½ cups fat-free plain yogurt
¼ cup fresh lemon juice
3 garlic cloves, minced
2 tablespoons minced peeled fresh ginger
1 tablespoon + 2 teaspoons paprika
2 teaspoons ground cumin

2 teaspoons curry powder (preferably Madras curry powder)
2½ pounds lean butterflied leg of lamb
1 teaspoon salt
¼ teaspoon freshly ground pepper

Combine the yogurt, lemon juice, garlic, ginger, paprika, cumin, and curry powder in a zip-close plastic bag; add the lamb. Squeeze out the air and seal the bag; turn to coat the lamb. Refrigerate, turning the bag occasionally, at least 2 hours or up to 24 hours.

Spray the grill rack with olive oil nonstick spray; prepare the grill for a medium fire using the direct method (see page 81).

Remove the lamb from the marinade; discard marinade. Sprinkle the lamb with the salt and pepper. Place the lamb on the grill rack and grill, turning once, until an instant-read thermometer inserted in the thickest part of the lamb registers 145°F for medium-rare, about 10 minutes on each side, or 160°F for medium, about 12 minutes on each side. Transfer the lamb to a cutting board and let stand, about 10 minutes. Cut the lamb into 16 slices.

PER SERVING (2 slices lamb): 208 Cal, 8 g Fat, 3 g Sat Fat, 0 g Trans Fat, 80 mg Chol, 379 mg Sod, 6 g Carb, 1 g Fib, 27 g Prot, 75 mg Calc. *POINTS* value: *5.*

**GRILLED LAMB WITH
PARSLEY AND MINT**

Grilled Lamb with Parsley and Mint

This is a classic early-spring recipe, ideal for the first outdoor grill of the season. For an interesting variation in flavor, add a tablespoon or two of minced fresh tarragon to the marinade. Parslied couscous and steamed carrots make delicious accompaniments to the lamb.

MAKES 6 SERVINGS

½ cup red-wine vinegar

¼ cup diced red onion

¼ cup minced fresh mint

¼ cup minced fresh parsley

¼ cup dry red wine

1 tablespoon + 1 teaspoon Dijon mustard

¼ teaspoon freshly ground pepper

1½ pounds lean butterflied leg of lamb

Combine the vinegar, onion, mint, parsley, wine, mustard, and pepper in a zip-close plastic bag; add the lamb. Squeeze out the air and seal the bag; turn to coat the lamb. Refrigerate for at least 2 hours or up to overnight.

Spray the grill rack with nonstick spray; prepare the grill for a medium-hot fire using the direct method (see page 81).

Drain the marinade into a small saucepan; boil, stirring constantly, for 3 minutes. Remove the marinade from the heat.

Place the lamb on the grill rack and grill, basting with the marinade and turning once, until an instant-read thermometer inserted in the thickest part of the lamb registers 145°F for medium-rare, about 10 minutes on each side, or 160°F for medium, about 12 minutes on each side. Transfer the lamb to a cutting board, spoon the cooked marinade over the lamb, and let stand, about 10 minutes. Cut into 12 slices.

PER SERVING (2 slices lamb): 156 Cal, 6 g Fat, 2 g Sat Fat, 0 g Trans Fat, 63 mg Chol, 136 mg Sod, 3 g Carb, 1 g Fib, 20 g Prot, 23 mg Calc. *POINTS* value: *3.*

Lamb Chops with Tomato Chutney

Lamb goes well with many types of chutney, but this is particularly satisfying with the combination of tomato, cool mint, and hot crushed red pepper. You can make the chutney up to 3 days ahead and store it, covered, in the refrigerator.

MAKES 4 SERVINGS

- 1 tablespoon + 1 teaspoon olive oil
- ½ cup chopped onion
- 2 garlic cloves, minced
- 4 small plum tomatoes, chopped
- ½ cup diced yellow bell pepper
- ½ teaspoon sugar
- ¼ teaspoon salt

- ¼ teaspoon freshly ground pepper
- 2 tablespoons minced fresh mint
- 2 tablespoons fresh lime juice
- ⅛–¼ teaspoon crushed red pepper
- 4 (5-ounce) lean loin lamb chops, ¾-inch thick

To make the chutney, heat the oil in a medium nonstick skillet over medium-high heat. Add the onion and garlic; cook, stirring frequently, until softened, about 2 minutes. Add the tomatoes, bell pepper, sugar, salt, and ground pepper; cook, stirring, until the bell pepper is crisp-tender, about 3 minutes. Transfer the vegetable mixture to a small bowl. Stir in the mint, lime juice, and crushed red pepper; set the chutney aside.

Spray the grill rack with nonstick spray; prepare the grill for a medium fire using the direct method (see page 81).

Place the chops on the grill rack and grill until an instant-read thermometer inserted in the thickest part of the chop registers 145°F for medium-rare, about 4½ minutes on each side, or 160°F for medium, about 5 minutes on each side. Serve the chops with the chutney.

PER SERVING (1 lamb chop and ½ cup chutney): 245 Cal, 13 g Fat, 4 g Sat Fat, 0 g Trans Fat, 81 mg Chol, 211 mg Sod, 5 g Carb, 1 g Fib, 26 g Prot, 29 mg Calc. *POINTS* value: *6.*

Walnut-Crusted Lamb Chops

Jalapeño jelly gives a delightful kick to these simple and delicious chops. It's also the secret to making the walnuts stick. You can substitute mint jelly for the spicy jalapeño jelly, if you prefer.

MAKES 4 SERVINGS

- **4 (5-ounce) lean loin lamb chops, 1½ inches thick**
- **1 tablespoon + 1 teaspoon jalapeño jelly**
- **1 garlic clove, finely minced**
- **⅛ teaspoon salt**
- **⅛ teaspoon freshly ground pepper**
- **2 tablespoons finely chopped walnuts**

Spray the grill rack with nonstick spray; prepare the grill for a medium fire using the direct method (see page 81).

Place the chops on the grill rack and grill until an instant-read thermometer inserted in the thickest part of the chop registers 145°F for medium-rare, about 4½ minutes on each side, or 160°F for medium, about 5 minutes on each side.

Meanwhile, combine the jelly, garlic, salt, and pepper in a small bowl. Transfer the chops to warm plates; with a pastry brush, coat the chops all over with the jelly mixture. Sprinkle the walnuts evenly over the chops to form a nut crust before serving.

PER SERVING (1 chop): 224 Cal, 10 g Fat, 3 g Sat Fat, 0 g Trans Fat, 81 mg Chol, 143 mg Sod, 5 g Carb, 0 g Fib, 26 g Prot, 21 mg Calc. **POINTS** value: **5.**

Poultry Power

✔ Grill-Roasted Tarragon Chicken

The secret to this juicy and flavorful golden bird is a basting sauce of broth and a hefty dose of vanilla extract. Fresh tarragon sprigs are slipped under the skin of each breast and in the cavity of the chicken, and the combination of tarragon and vanilla is just superb.

MAKES 8 SERVINGS

- 1 (3-pound) whole chicken
- 1 garlic clove
- 6–8 fresh tarragon sprigs
- 1/4 teaspoon salt
- 1/2 teaspoon freshly ground pepper
- 1/4 cup reduced-sodium chicken broth
- 2 tablespoons vanilla extract

Spray the grill rack with nonstick spray; prepare the grill for a medium fire using the indirect method (see page 81).

Rinse the chicken thoroughly inside and out; pat dry with paper towels. Discard the giblets and remove any visible fat. Rub the chicken cavity with the garlic clove. Gently loosen the breast skin with your fingers and insert a tarragon sprig under the skin of each breast. Stuff the remaining sprigs in the chicken cavity. Tuck the wings under the breast and tie the legs together with kitchen twine. Sprinkle the chicken all over with the salt and pepper.

To make the basting sauce, combine the broth and vanilla in a small cup.

Place the chicken on the grill rack, breast-side up, cover the grill and cook, with all grill vents open, brushing every 10 minutes with the basting sauce, until an instant-read thermometer inserted in a thigh registers 180°F, about 1 hour. Transfer the chicken to a platter and let rest about 10 minutes; remove the twine. Remove the skin before eating.

PER SERVING (1/8 of chicken): 121 Cal, 4 g Fat, 1 g Sat Fat, 0 g Trans Fat, 50 mg Chol, 118 mg Sod, 1 g Carb, 0 g Fib, 16 g Prot, 10 mg Calc. *POINTS* value: *3.*

GRILL-ROASTED
TARRAGON CHICKEN

Whole Grilled Chicken with Rosemary

Delicious and incredibly simple to make—what more could you ask for? For added flavor and fragrance, sprinkle a teaspoon or two of dried rosemary over the hot coals before you begin grilling the bird.

MAKES 6 SERVINGS

1 (3½-pound) whole chicken	2 teaspoons salt
2 garlic cloves, minced	1 teaspoon freshly
1 tablespoon minced fresh	ground pepper
rosemary, or 1 teaspoon dried,	1 lemon, halved
crumbled rosemary	

Spray the grill rack with nonstick spray; prepare the grill for a medium fire using the indirect method (see page 81).

Rinse the chicken thoroughly inside and out; pat dry with paper towels. Discard the giblets and remove any visible fat. Rub the chicken inside and out with the garlic, rosemary, salt, and pepper. Squeeze the lemon juice over the chicken and place the lemon halves in the chicken cavity. Tuck the wings under the breast and tie the legs together with kitchen twine.

Place the chicken on the grill rack, breast-side up, cover the grill and cook, with all grill vents open, until an instant-read thermometer inserted in a thigh registers 180°F, about 1 hour. Transfer the chicken to a platter and let rest about 10 minutes; remove the twine. Remove the skin before eating.

PER SERVING (⅙ of chicken): 168 Cal, 6 g Fat, 2 g Sat Fat, 0 g Trans Fat, 76 mg Chol, 808 mg Sod, 3 g Carb, 0 g Fib, 25 g Prot, 36 mg Calc. **POINTS** value: **4.**

Chipotle Chicken Breasts with Orange-Scallion Relish

This flavorful chicken is marinated with chipotles en adobo, which are ripened, dried, and smoked jalapeño peppers packed in a spicy tomato sauce. The chipotles give a peppery, Southwestern flavor to the chicken, which is cooled by the citrus relish.

MAKES 4 SERVINGS

- 2 chipotles en adobo, minced
- 1 tablespoon grated orange zest
- Grated zest and juice of ½ lemon
- 2 teaspoons sugar
- 1 tablespoon olive oil
- 2 (¾-pound) bone-in chicken breast halves, skinned and cut in half the short way

- 3 oranges, peeled and chopped, juices reserved
- 4 scallions, green part only, chopped
- 1 tablespoon rinsed drained capers
- 1 teaspoon salt

Combine the chipotles, orange zest, lemon zest, lemon juice, sugar, and oil in a zip-close plastic bag; add the chicken. Squeeze out the air and seal the bag; turn to coat the chicken. Refrigerate, turning the bag occasionally, at least 4 hours or up to overnight.

Spray the grill rack with nonstick spray; prepare the grill for a medium-hot fire using the direct method (see page 81).

To make the relish, combine the chopped oranges and reserved juices, the scallions, and capers in a medium bowl; mix well and set aside.

Lift the chicken from the marinade and sprinkle with the salt. Discard the marinade. Place the chicken on the grill rack and grill until the chicken is well marked and an instant-read thermometer inserted in a breast registers 170°F, 10–12 minutes on each side. Serve the chicken with the relish.

PER SERVING (1 piece chicken with about ⅓ cup relish): 150 Cal, 3 g Fat, 1 g Sat Fat, 0 g Trans Fat, 42 mg Chol, 758 mg Sod, 14 g Carb, 3 g Fib, 16 g Prot, 60 mg Calc.
POINTS value: *3.*

**GREEK CHICKEN
WITH PITAS
AND TZATZIKI**

Greek Chicken with Pitas and Tzatziki

The key to great tzatziki is using yogurt cheese instead of plain yogurt. Allow at least 1½ hours to strain the yogurt. The longer it is allowed to drain, the thicker (and creamier) the yogurt becomes.

MAKES 4 SERVINGS

4 small garlic cloves, minced

5 teaspoons extra-virgin olive oil

1 teaspoon dried oregano

4 (¼-pound) skinless boneless chicken breast halves

½ cup yogurt cheese (see TIP page 102, but start with 1 cup yogurt)

½ cucumber, peeled, seeded, grated, and squeezed dry

1 tablespoon chopped fresh mint

¾ teaspoon salt

¼ teaspoon freshly ground pepper

2 (6-inch) pita breads

Combine 3 of the garlic cloves, 3 teaspoons of the oil, and the oregano in a zip-close plastic bag; add the chicken. Squeeze out the air and seal the bag; turn to coat the chicken. Refrigerate, turning the bag occasionally, at least 1½ hours or up to overnight.

Spray the grill rack with nonstick spray; prepare the grill for a medium-hot fire using the direct method (see page 81).

To make the tzatziki, combine the yogurt cheese, the remaining garlic clove and 2 teaspoons oil, the cucumber, mint, ¼ teaspoon of the salt, and ⅛ teaspoon of the pepper in a medium bowl; mix well and set aside.

Lift the chicken from the marinade and sprinkle with the remaining ½ teaspoon salt and ⅛ teaspoon pepper. Discard the marinade. Place the chicken on the grill rack and grill until well marked and an instant-read thermometer inserted in a breast registers 170°F, 5–6 minutes on each side. Transfer the chicken to a plate and cover lightly with foil to keep warm.

Place the pita breads on the grill rack and grill until toasted, about 2 minutes on each side. Cut each pita in fourths. Serve the chicken with pita and tzatziki.

PER SERVING (1 piece chicken, 2 pieces pita, and ¼ cup tzatziki): 277 Cal, 7 g Fat, 2 g Sat Fat, 0 g Trans Fat, 70 mg Chol, 689 mg Sod, 20 g Carb, 1 g Fib, 31 g Prot, 165 mg Calc.
POINTS value: *6.*

Grilled Chicken Cordon Bleu

Here's an easy, light version of a usually time-consuming, rich classic. Instead of stuffing pounded chicken breasts with ham and cheese, then coating with crumbs and frying, we simply grill the chicken, top it with a little ham and cheese then cover the grill to melt the cheese.

MAKES 4 SERVINGS

4 (¼-pound) skinless boneless chicken breast halves
2 teaspoons olive oil
⅛ teaspoon salt
¼ teaspoon freshly ground pepper

2 teaspoons Dijon mustard
¼ pound deli-sliced ham (4 slices)
2 ounces thinly sliced reduced-fat Swiss cheese (4 slices)

Spray the grill rack with nonstick spray; prepare the grill for a medium-hot fire using the direct method (see page 81).

Rub the chicken with the oil, then sprinkle with the salt and pepper. Place the chicken on the grill rack and grill 4 minutes. Turn the chicken and brush each breast half with ½ teaspoon of the mustard. Top each with 1 slice of the ham and 1 slice of the cheese. Cover the grill and grill until an instant-read thermometer inserted in a breast registers 170°F, the ham is hot, and the cheese melts, 7–8 minutes longer.

PER SERVING (1 piece chicken): 249 Cal, 11 g Fat, 4 g Sat Fat, 0 g Trans Fat, 94 mg Chol, 569 mg Sod, 1 g Carb, 0 g Fib, 35 g Prot, 114 mg Calc. *POINTS* value: *6.*

TIP Try serving the chicken with grilled vegetables, such as zucchini and yellow squash, sprinkled with a fresh squeeze of lemon.

Chicken with Lemon, Ginger, and Basil

Chicken dishes are often delicious cold and this dish is no exception. If you don't eat it right away, cover and refrigerate it for up to 2 days, then let it sit at room temperature for 20 minutes before serving.

MAKES 4 SERVINGS

- 1 teaspoon grated lemon zest
- 3 tablespoons fresh lemon juice
- 1 tablespoon + 1 teaspoon canola oil
- 2 garlic cloves, minced
- 1 teaspoon minced peeled fresh ginger
- 4 (¼-pound) skinless boneless chicken breast halves

- ½ teaspoon salt
- ¼ teaspoon freshly ground pepper
- 1 large red bell pepper, seeded and cut into thin strips
- 2 tablespoons coarsely chopped fresh basil

Combine the lemon zest, lemon juice, oil, garlic, and ginger in a zip-close plastic bag; add the chicken. Squeeze out the air and seal the bag; turn to coat the chicken. Refrigerate, turning the bag occasionally, at least 1 hour or up to overnight.

Spray the grill rack with nonstick spray; prepare the grill for a medium fire using the direct method (see page 81). Spray a grill basket with nonstick spray.

Lift the chicken from the marinade. Pour the marinade into a small saucepan and boil, stirring constantly, 3 minutes.

Sprinkle the chicken with the salt and ground pepper. Place it on the grill rack, and grill, basting with the marinade, until an instant-read thermometer inserted in a breast registers 170°F, about 5 minutes on each side. Grill the pepper strips in the grill basket until slightly charred, about 6 minutes.

Serve the chicken with the pepper strips and sprinkle with the basil.

PER SERVING (1 piece chicken and ¼ of pepper strips): 200 Cal, 8 g Fat, 1 g Sat Fat, 0 g Trans Fat, 72 mg Chol, 338 mg Sod, 5 g Carb, 1 g Fib, 27 g Prot, 35 mg Calc. **POINTS** value: **4.**

TIP The zest of the lemon is the peel without any of the pith (white membrane). To grate zest, use a zester or the fine side of a vegetable grater.

Curry-Marinated Chicken Kebabs

Curry subtly flavors both the chicken and apples here. Increase the amount of curry powder if you'd like a more intense flavor. You can use metal or wooden skewers for these kebabs, but if using wooden skewers, be sure to soak them in water for 30 minutes before putting them on the grill.

MAKES 4 SERVINGS

½ cup apple juice

1 tablespoon + 1½ teaspoons fresh lemon juice

1 tablespoon honey

2 teaspoons olive oil

1 teaspoon curry powder

⅛ teaspoon salt

Pinch freshly ground pepper

¾ pound skinless boneless chicken breast, cut into 24 pieces

3 medium apples, cored and cut into 48 (¾-inch) pieces

2 cups hot cooked white rice

Spray the grill rack with nonstick spray; prepare the grill for a medium fire using the direct method (see page 81).

To make the marinade, combine the apple and lemon juices, the honey, oil, curry powder, salt, and pepper in a zip-close plastic bag. Add the chicken pieces. Squeeze out the air and seal the bag; turn to coat the chicken. Refrigerate, turning the bag occasionally, at least 30 minutes or up to overnight. Remove the chicken pieces from the marinade.

Pour the marinade into a small saucepan and boil, stirring often, 3 minutes.

Thread 6 chicken pieces onto each of 4 (12-inch) metal or wooden skewers. Thread 6 apple pieces onto each of 8 more 12-inch metal or wooden skewers. Brush the apple skewers with the cooked marinade and place the chicken and apple skewers on the grill rack. Grill, turning occasionally, until the chicken is cooked through and apples are tender, 5–7 minutes. Serve kebabs with the rice.

PER SERVING (½ cup rice, 1 chicken kebab, and 2 apple kebabs): 289 Cal, 3 g Fat, 1 g Sat Fat, 0 g Trans Fat, 47 mg Chol, 116 mg Sod, 47 g Carb, 3 g Fib, 20 g Prot, 29 mg Calc. *POINTS* value: *5.*

Bacon-Wrapped Chicken Thighs

This delicious dish gets plenty of flavor from a simple marinade that includes vinegar, which helps tenderize the meat much like yogurt does for a tandoori or wine does for a steak.

MAKES 4 SERVINGS

1 large shallot, finely chopped

2 tablespoons red-wine vinegar

2 tablespoons reduced-sodium soy sauce

2 teaspoons chopped fresh thyme, or ½ teaspoon dried

4 (¼-pound) skinless boneless chicken thighs

8 slices turkey bacon

Combine the shallot, vinegar, soy sauce, and thyme in a zip-close plastic bag; add the chicken. Squeeze out the air and seal the bag; turn to coat chicken. Refrigerate, turning the bag occasionally, at least 1 hour or up to overnight.

Spray the grill rack with nonstick spray; prepare the grill for a medium-hot fire using the direct method (see page 81).

Lift the chicken from the marinade and pat dry with paper towels. Discard the marinade. Wrap each chicken thigh with 2 slices of the bacon. Place on the grill rack, cover the grill, and grill until the bacon is crisp and the chicken is cooked through, 6–7 minutes on each side.

PER SERVING (1 chicken thigh): 175 Cal, 10 g Fat, 3 g Sat Fat, 0 g Trans Fat, 58 mg Chol, 486 mg Sod, 0 g Carb, 0 g Fib, 18 g Prot, 21 mg Calc. *POINTS* value: *4.*

TIP Be sure to place the bacon-wrapped chicken seam-side down on the grill rack to allow the bacon edges to seal and keep the chicken moist.

Chicken Teriyaki with Udon

Here is Japan's answer to our cure-all chicken soup—a bowlful of fragrant broth, thick wheat udon noodles, and delicately flavored grilled chicken pieces. You can find udon in Asian markets in either fresh or dried form.

MAKES 4 SERVINGS

- 3 tablespoons + 1 teaspoon reduced-sodium soy sauce
- 2 tablespoons mirin (rice wine)
- 1 tablespoon honey
- 4 (¼-pound) skinless boneless chicken thighs
- 6 ounces udon noodles

- 2 teaspoons Asian (dark) sesame oil
- 2 scallions, chopped
- 1 tablespoon grated peeled fresh ginger
- 1½ cups reduced-sodium chicken broth

Combine the 3 tablespoons soy sauce, the mirin, and honey in a zip-close plastic bag; add the chicken. Squeeze out the air and seal the bag; turn to coat the chicken. Refrigerate, turning the bag occasionally, at least 30 minutes or up to overnight.

Meanwhile, bring a pot of water to a boil. Add the noodles and cook according to package directions; drain. Heat the oil in a medium saucepan over medium-high heat. Add the scallions and ginger; cook, stirring constantly, until fragrant, about 1 minute. Add the broth and the remaining 1 teaspoon soy sauce; bring to a boil and cook 2 minutes. Add the noodles and return to a simmer. Remove from the heat and cover to keep warm.

Spray the grill rack with nonstick spray; prepare the grill for a medium-hot fire using the direct method (see page 81).

Lift the chicken from the marinade and place on the grill rack. Discard the marinade. Grill the chicken until well marked and cooked through, 6–7 minutes on each side. Transfer the chicken to a cutting board and slice. Divide the broth and noodles among 4 bowls; top each with 1 sliced chicken thigh.

PER SERVING (½ cup noodles and broth with 1 sliced chicken thigh): 298 Cal, 9 g Fat, 2 g Sat Fat, 0 g Trans Fat, 43 mg Chol, 368 mg Sod, 33 g Carb, 3 g Fib, 22 g Prot, 43 mg Calc. **POINTS** value: **6.**

GRILLED CHICKEN AND
AVOCADO QUESADILLAS

Grilled Chicken and Avocado Quesadillas

These easy-to-assemble quesadillas make a quick weeknight meal or great party fare. You can double the recipe and turn the quesadillas into canapés by simply cutting each into 4 wedges with a sharp knife. If you can stand the heat, serve with pickled sliced jalapeños.

MAKES 4 SERVINGS

- 2 onions, thinly sliced
- 1 jalapeño pepper, seeded and finely chopped (wear gloves to prevent irritation)
- 4 (8-inch) fat-free flour tortillas
- ½ ripe Haas avocado, pitted, peeled, and pureed
- ¾ cup reduced-fat Mexican cheese blend
- ½ (10-ounce) package carved roasted skinless chicken breast pieces, cut into smaller pieces
- 2 tablespoons chopped fresh cilantro

Spray the grill rack with nonstick spray; prepare the grill for a medium-hot fire using the direct method (see page 81).

Spray a large nonstick skillet with nonstick spray and set over medium heat. Add the onions and jalapeño; cook, stirring occasionally, until golden, 8–10 minutes. Remove the skillet from the heat and let cool about 5 minutes.

Place the tortillas on a work surface. Spread half of each tortilla with one-fourth of the avocado. Then top each with 3 tablespoons cheese, one-fourth of the onion mixture, one-fourth of the chicken, and one-fourth of the cilantro. Fold the top half of the tortilla over the filling to form a semi-circle; press the edges together lightly to seal.

Place the quesadillas on the grill rack and grill until the cheese melts, the filling is hot, and the tortillas are crisp, 3–4 minutes on each side.

PER SERVING (1 quesadilla): 323 Cal, 9 g Fat, 3 g Sat Fat, 0 g Trans Fat, 41 mg Chol, 652 mg Sod, 38 g Carb, 3 g Fib, 22 g Prot, 213 mg Calc. *POINTS* value: *7.*

TIP A long-handled, wide metal spatula is an indispensable tool when making quesadillas on the grill. You can slide it underneath the quesadillas and turn them over with ease.

Grilled Drumsticks with Orange Glaze

Nothing could be easier to make than these drumsticks! It takes only minutes to prepare the delicious glaze; then it's just a matter of firing up the grill for some very good eating. They go beautifully with the equally delicious Grilled Sweet Potatoes with Lime (page 144).

MAKES 4 SERVINGS

¼ cup orange marmalade spreadable fruit

1 tablespoon + 1 teaspoon minced fresh thyme leaves

½ teaspoon salt

½ teaspoon extra-virgin olive oil

¼ teaspoon freshly ground pepper

4 (3-ounce) skinless chicken drumsticks

Spray the grill rack with nonstick spray; prepare the grill for a medium fire using the direct method (see page 81).

Combine the spreadable fruit, thyme, salt, oil, and pepper in a small bowl; brush 1 tablespoon of the glaze on each drumstick.

Place the drumsticks on the grill rack, and grill, turning occasionally and brushing with the remaining glaze, until an instant-read thermometer inserted in a drumstick registers 180°F, 10–12 minutes.

PER SERVING (1 drumstick): 121 Cal, 3 g Fat, 1 g Sat Fat, 0 g Trans Fat, 40 mg Chol, 314 mg Sod, 11 g Carb, 0 g Fib, 12 g Prot, 14 mg Calc. *POINTS* value: *3.*

TIP If you prefer, broil the chicken: Spray the broiler rack with nonstick spray and preheat the broiler. Broil the chicken 4 inches from the heat, turning occasionally and brushing with the remaining glaze, until an instant-read thermometer inserted in a drumstick registers 180°F, 10–12 minutes.

Grilled Whole Turkey Breast

Guests who have never tasted turkey roasted on the grill may be a little dubious, but this smoky and delicious herbed breast may change their minds. Try it next Thanksgiving—or anytime you're entertaining a crowd. Serve it with Sweet-and-Spicy Sweet Potatoes (page 145) and Minted Green Beans (page 130).

MAKES 12 SERVINGS

2 garlic cloves, minced

1 tablespoon dried sage leaves, crumbled

1 teaspoon salt

½ teaspoon freshly ground pepper

1 (3-pound) skinless bone-in turkey breast

Spray the grill rack with nonstick spray; prepare the grill for a medium fire using the indirect method (see page 81).

Combine the garlic, sage, salt, and pepper in a small bowl. Rub the turkey breast all over with the mixture.

Place the turkey on the grill rack, and grill, covered, with all of the grill vents open, until an instant-read thermometer inserted in a thigh registers 180°F, about 50 minutes.

Transfer the turkey to a carving board and let stand about 10 minutes. Slice the turkey into 24 slices.

PER SERVING (2 slices turkey): 116 Cal, 1 g Fat, 0 g Sat Fat, 0 g Trans Fat, 71 mg Chol, 228 mg Sod, 0 g Carb, 0 g Fib, 26 g Prot, 15 mg Calc. **POINTS** value: **2.**

Grilled Turkey Roulade

This attractive roulade is filled with a fragrant and colorful combination of olives, sun-dried tomatoes, parsley, rosemary, and lemon zest. You might like to add a few long slices of zucchini and thick slices of red onion to the grill during the last few minutes of cooking and serve them alongside.

MAKES 6 SERVINGS

16 sun-dried tomatoes (not oil-packed), about ⅔ cup
20 pitted kalamata olives, minced
¼ cup chopped fresh parsley
¼ cup plain dry bread crumbs
1 tablespoon + 1 teaspoon extra-virgin olive oil
2 teaspoons grated lemon zest
1½ teaspoons chopped fresh rosemary
1 (1½-pound) piece skinless boneless turkey breast
½ teaspoon salt
¼ teaspoon freshly ground pepper

Spray the grill rack with nonstick spray; prepare the grill for a medium-hot fire using the indirect method (see page 81).

Combine the sun-dried tomatoes with enough boiling water to cover in a small bowl. Let stand until softened, about 15 minutes. Drain the tomatoes then finely chop. Transfer the tomatoes to a medium bowl. Add the olives, parsley, bread crumbs, the 1 tablespoon oil, the lemon zest, and rosemary; mix well.

With a sharp knife, butterfly the turkey breast piece by cutting through it horizontally and leaving a ¾-inch hinge. Lightly pound the turkey to a ¼-inch thickness. Sprinkle the cut side of the turkey with ¼ teaspoon of the salt and ⅛ teaspoon of the pepper. Press the tomato mixture onto the turkey leaving a ½-inch border all around. Roll up the turkey, jelly-roll style, and secure with kitchen string. Rub the turkey with the remaining 1 teaspoon oil and sprinkle with the remaining ¼ teaspoon salt and ⅛ teaspoon pepper.

Place the turkey roulade on the grill rack, cover the grill, and cook, turning every 10 minutes, until an instant-read thermometer inserted in the center registers 170°F, 60–70 minutes.

Transfer the turkey to a carving board and let stand about 10 minutes. Remove the string and cut into 12 slices.

PER SERVING (2 slices turkey): 199 Cal, 6 g Fat, 1 g Sat Fat, 0 g Trans Fat, 75 mg Chol, 529 mg Sod, 8 g Carb, 1 g Fib, 28 g Prot, 46 mg Calc. *POINTS* value: *4.*

Turkey Spiedini

These Italian kebabs are easy, quick, full of flavor, attractive, and fun—few dishes can boast so many attributes.

MAKES 6 SERVINGS

⅓ cup dry red wine

2 tablespoons red-wine vinegar

1 tablespoon extra-virgin olive oil

3 garlic cloves, minced

1 tablespoon chopped fresh oregano, or 1½ teaspoons dried

1 teaspoon chopped fresh thyme, or ½ teaspoon dried

1½ pounds skinless boneless turkey breast, cut into 30 pieces

18 small fresh white mushrooms

12 cherry tomatoes

¾ teaspoon salt

¼ teaspoon freshly ground pepper

Combine the wine, vinegar, oil, garlic, oregano, and thyme in a zip-close plastic bag; add the turkey pieces. Squeeze out the air and seal the bag; turn to coat the turkey. Refrigerate, turning the bag occasionally, about 1 hour.

Spray the grill rack with nonstick spray; prepare the grill for a medium-hot fire using the direct method (see page 81).

Lift the turkey from the marinade and discard the marinade. On each of 6 (12-inch) skewers, alternate 5 turkey pieces, 3 mushrooms, and 2 tomatoes. Sprinkle the kebabs with the salt and pepper.

Place the skewers on the grill rack. Cover the grill and cook until the turkey is cooked through and the vegetables are tender, about 10 minutes on each side.

PER SERVING (1 skewer): 144 Cal, 2 g Fat, 0 g Sat Fat, 0 g Trans Fat, 75 mg Chol, 348 mg Sod, 3 g Carb, 1 g Fib, 28 g Prot, 19 mg Calc. **POINTS** value: **3.**

TIP When grilling food on a skewer, position each bit of food about ¼ inch apart to ensure that it will cook evenly.

Turkey Cutlets with Cranberry Salsa

This is a unique way to cook turkey for a small, casual Thanksgiving celebration—or for any dinner party, for that matter. The chunky fruit salsa can be made up to a month ahead and frozen. To defrost, place it in the refrigerator overnight.

MAKES 4 SERVINGS

1 cup fresh or frozen cranberries

½ cup chopped scallions

1 small orange, peeled and coarsely chopped

2 teaspoons sugar

2 tablespoons fresh orange juice

1 tablespoon + 1 teaspoon olive oil

1 tablespoon minced fresh thyme

½ teaspoon salt

¼ teaspoon freshly ground pepper

4 (5-ounce) turkey cutlets, pounded ¼ inch thick

Combine the cranberries, scallions, orange, and sugar in a food processor; process until coarsely chopped, about 1 minute. Transfer to a serving bowl and set aside.

Combine the orange juice, oil, thyme, salt, and pepper in a zip-close plastic bag; add the turkey cutlets. Squeeze out the air and seal the bag; turn to coat the turkey. Refrigerate, turning the bag occasionally, about 30 minutes.

Spray the grill rack with nonstick spray; prepare the grill for a medium fire using the direct method (see page 81).

Place the turkey cutlets on the grill rack and grill until cooked through, about 3 minutes on each side. Serve the cutlets with the salsa.

PER SERVING (1 turkey cutlet with ¼ cup salsa): 237 Cal, 5 g Fat, 1 g Sat Fat, 0 g Trans Fat, 94 mg Chol, 335 mg Sod, 11 g Carb, 2 g Fib, 35 g Prot, 46 mg Calc. *POINTS* value: *5.*

Turkey Burgers with Bulgur and Mint

With bulgur boosting their fiber, these juicy, Middle Eastern-spiced burgers are a deliciously healthful alternative to the usual beef variety. Serve each burger with a couple of tomato slices in a whole-wheat pita, split and grilled, and deduct the pita from your **weekly POINTS Allowance.**

MAKES 4 SERVINGS

¾ **pound ground skinless turkey breast**

¾ **cup chopped tomato**

½ **cup cooked bulgur**

¼ **cup chopped scallions**

¼ **cup plain fat-free yogurt**

2 **teaspoons minced fresh mint**

½ **teaspoon ground cumin**

¼ **teaspoon salt**

Spray the grill rack with nonstick spray; prepare the grill for a medium fire using the direct method (see page 81).

Combine the turkey, tomato, bulgur, scallions, yogurt, mint, cumin, and salt in a large bowl. Lightly moisten hands; shape the mixture into 4 equal patties.

Place the patties on the grill and grill until an instant-read thermometer inserted in the side of a burger registers 165°F, about 5 minutes on each side.

PER SERVING (1 burger): 127 Cal, 1 g Fat, 0 g Sat Fat, 0 g Trans Fat, 56 mg Chol, 195 mg Sod, 7 g Carb, 2 g Fib, 22 g Prot, 39 mg Calc. **POINTS** value: **2.**

COOKING METHODS

Food is grilled using one of two different methods of cooking: direct or indirect. We specify the grilling method to be used in every recipe in this book.

The Direct Method

Food is placed directly above the heat source of either the gas or charcoal grill. It is the most common way of grilling food. For gas grills, simply heat to the desired temperature. For charcoal grills, spread the coals in the middle of the grill and heat them to the temperature specified in the recipe. Place the food on the grill rack, 4 to 5 inches from the heat source, directly above the coals. The direct method cooks food relatively quickly, resulting in more browning on the outside of the food. Direct cooking is best suited for smaller pieces of food such as kebabs, steaks, chops, burgers, or vegetables.

The Indirect Method

For gas grills, light only one burner, place the food over the unlit burner, close the lid, and grill. For charcoal grills, mound the charcoal on one side of the grill and cook the food over the unheated side of the grill. Or place a drip pan slightly larger than the food being cooked in the middle of the bottom of the grill (a foil pie pan makes a perfect drip pan). Spread the charcoal briquettes evenly around the drip pan, position the grill rack 4 to 5 inches above the pan, and place the food on the grill rack directly over the drip pan. The indirect method is the best way to cook larger, thicker items such as whole roasts, chickens, or turkeys, or other large cuts of meat.

Mushroom-Stuffed Cornish Hens

Cornish hens are a perfect dish for dinner parties. Not only are they elegant and flavorful, each serving is just the right size to make each guest feel special.

MAKES 4 SERVINGS

- 1 medium onion, diced
- ½ cup chopped fresh porcini (cèpe) mushrooms
- ½ cup chopped fresh shiitake mushrooms
- ½ cup chopped fresh cremini mushrooms
- 1 garlic clove, minced

- 1 tablespoon minced fresh parsley
- 1 tablespoon red-wine vinegar
- 1 tablespoon balsamic vinegar
- ½ teaspoon ground thyme
- 2 (1-pound) Cornish game hens
- ½ teaspoon salt
- ½ teaspoon freshly ground pepper

Spray the grill rack with nonstick spray; prepare the grill for a medium fire using the indirect method (see page 81).

Spray a medium skillet with nonstick spray and set over medium heat; add the onion and cook, stirring constantly, until translucent, about 3 minutes. Add all the mushrooms and the garlic; cook, stirring constantly, about 5 minutes. Stir in the parsley, red-wine vinegar, balsamic vinegar, and thyme; cook, stirring constantly, until the mushrooms are softened, about 6 minutes. Set aside and allow to cool completely.

Rinse the hens thoroughly inside and out; pat dry with paper towels. Discard the giblets and remove any visible fat. Sprinkle the hens inside and out with the salt and pepper; fill each of the hen cavities with half of the mushroom stuffing. Tuck the wings under the breast, close the cavities with skewers, and tie the legs together with kitchen twine.

Place the hens on the grill rack and grill, covered, with all the grill vents open, until an instant-read thermometer inserted in a thigh registers 180°F, about 40 minutes. Let stand 10 minutes.

Remove the skewers and twine; cut the hens in half with poultry shears. Remove the skin before eating.

PER SERVING (½ stuffed hen): 143 Cal, 4 g Fat, 1 g Sat Fat, 0 g Trans Fat, 97 mg Chol, 352 mg Sod, 4 g Carb, 1 g Fib, 23 g Prot, 26 mg Calc. *POINTS* value: *3.*

Beer-Marinated Grilled Cornish Hens

In order to grill a whole Cornish hen faster, it's best to split it open so that it will lie flat on the grill and cook evenly. The method we use to splay hens open is called spatchcocking; follow our simple directions in Step 1.

MAKES 4 SERVINGS

2 (1½-pound) Cornish game hens
1 (12-ounce) bottle dark beer
Grated zest and juice of 1 lemon
2 garlic cloves, minced
1 tablespoon reduced-sodium soy sauce
1 teaspoon Asian (dark) sesame oil
1 teaspoon ground cumin
1 teaspoon dried oregano
¾ teaspoon salt
¼ teaspoon freshly ground pepper

To spatchcock the hens, with a sharp knife or poultry shears, remove the wings from the hens at the first joint. Then remove the backbone and spread the hens open, like a book, skin-side down. Use a paring knife and cut along each side of the breastbone. Run your thumbs along both sides of the breastbone and pull the white cartilage out, so that the hens can lie flat. Prick the hens all over with the tip of a knife.

Combine the beer, lemon zest, lemon juice, garlic, soy sauce, oil, cumin, and oregano in a zip-close plastic bag; add the hens. Squeeze out the air and seal the bag; turn to coat the hens. Refrigerate, turning the bag occasionally, at least 4 hours or up to overnight.

Spray the grill rack with nonstick spray; prepare the grill for a medium fire using the direct method (see page 81).

Lift the hens from the marinade and rub the salt and pepper under the skin. Discard the marinade. Place the hens on the grill rack and grill, skin-side down, 15 minutes, moving them to the edge of the grill if they brown too rapidly. With tongs, turn the birds skin-side up, and grill 15 minutes more. Turn again and grill until an instant-read thermometer inserted in a thigh registers 180°F, about 5 minutes longer. Remove the skin before eating.

PER SERVING (½ hen): 191 Cal, 6 g Fat, 1 g Sat Fat, 0 g Trans Fat, 146 mg Chol, 561 mg Sod, 1 g Carb, 0 g Fib, 32 g Prot, 22 mg Calc. **POINTS** value: **4.**

CORNISH HENS WITH
SWEET AND FRUITY GLAZE

Cornish Hens with Sweet and Fruity Glaze

These delicate little birds are equally delectable grilled in advance and served cold, a day or two later. Kale with Garlic and Balsamic (page 131) makes a perfect accompaniment. Garnish the hens with rosemary sprigs.

MAKES 4 SERVINGS

- ¼ cup reduced-sodium chicken broth
- 2 tablespoons raspberry vinegar
- 1 tablespoon seedless raspberry jam
- 2 teaspoons fresh rosemary, chopped
- ½ teaspoon coarsely ground black pepper
- Tiny pinch ground cloves
- 1 tablespoon canola oil
- 2 (1-pound) Cornish game hens

Combine the broth, vinegar, jam, rosemary, pepper, and cloves in a small saucepan; cook over medium heat, stirring frequently, until the jam has dissolved. Reserve half of the glaze; cover and refrigerate. Add the oil to the remaining half.

To spatchcock the hens, with a sharp knife or poultry shears, remove the wings from the hens at the first joint. Then remove the backbone and spread the hens open, like a book, skin-side down. Use a paring knife and cut along each side of the breastbone. Run your thumbs along both sides of the breastbone and pull the white cartilage out, so that the hens lie flat. Prick the hens all over with the tip of a knife; place in a large dish. Brush the glaze with oil over the hens. Cover the dish and refrigerate overnight.

Spray the grill rack with nonstick spray; prepare the grill for a medium fire using the direct method (see page 81).

Place the hens on the grill rack and grill, skin-side down, for 10 minutes, moving them to the edge of the grill if they brown too rapidly. With tongs, turn the birds skin-side up, and grill 15 minutes more. Turn again and grill until an instant-read thermometer inserted in a thigh registers 180°F, about 5 minutes longer. Remove the skin before eating. Warm the reserved glaze, and serve it with the grilled hens.

PER SERVING (½ hen with 1 tablespoon glaze): 169 Cal, 7 g Fat, 1 g Sat Fat, 0 g Trans Fat, 97 mg Chol, 97 mg Sod, 4 g Carb, 0 g Fib, 22 g Prot, 16 mg Calc. *POINTS* value: *4.*

Capon with Mole Sauce

Mexican mole sauce makes a spicy and delicious sauce for succulent capon, which cooks beautifully, covered, on the grill.

MAKES 20 SERVINGS

- 1 (8-pound) capon
- 1 small orange, quartered
- 2 teaspoons chili powder
- 1 teaspoon dried oregano
- ½ teaspoon cumin seeds
- 1 teaspoon canola oil
- ½ cup chopped onion
- 2 garlic cloves, minced
- 1½ cups low-sodium chicken broth

- 1 tablespoon tomato paste
- 1–3 teaspoons chopped chipotles en adobo
- 1 tablespoon + 1 teaspoon unsweetened cocoa powder
- 1 teaspoon cornmeal
- ½ teaspoon cinnamon
- ½ teaspoon ground anise seeds

Spray the grill rack with nonstick spray; prepare the grill for a hot fire using the indirect method (see page 81).

Discard the giblets from the capon and stuff the cavity with the orange quarters. Combine the chili powder, oregano, and cumin in a small bowl. Sprinkle all but 1 teaspoon of the spice mixture into the capon cavity. Tuck the wings under the breast and tie the legs together with kitchen twine. Rub the outside of the bird with the remaining spice mixture. Place it in a roasting pan.

Place roasting pan on grill rack. Cover grill and cook, with all grill vents open, 1 hour. Baste with pan juices; cover, and grill until an instant-read thermometer inserted in a thigh registers 180°F, about 30 minutes more.

Meanwhile, to make the sauce, heat the oil in a medium nonstick saucepan. Add the onion and garlic; cook, stirring frequently, until golden, about 7 minutes. Whisk in the broth, tomato paste, chipotles, cocoa, cornmeal, cinnamon, and anise until smooth; bring to a boil, stirring constantly. Reduce the heat and simmer, stirring often, about 15 minutes.

Remove the capon from the grill; cover loosely with foil and let stand 15 minutes. Carve into 20 slices. Remove the skin before eating. Serve with the sauce on the side.

PER SERVING (1 slice capon, 1 tablespoon sauce): 118 Cal, 5 g Fat, 1 g Sat Fat, 0 g Trans Fat, 50 mg Chol, 74 mg Sod, 1 g Carb, 0 g Fib, 17 g Prot, 17 mg Calc. *POINTS* value: *3.*

Duck Breasts with Spicy Apricot Glaze

Fruit and duck are the perfect combination—think Duck à L'Orange. Our fruit of choice is apricot, but you can substitute black cherry preserves for the apricot, if you prefer. Fresh duck is available from late spring to early winter. Frozen duck is available year round. Substitute skinless boneless turkey or chicken breasts, if you like.

MAKES 4 SERVINGS

- 3 tablespoons apricot preserves
- 1 tablespoon fresh lemon juice
- ¼ teaspoon crushed red pepper
- 4 (5–6-ounce) skinless boneless duck breasts
- 1 teaspoon ground coriander
- ¾ teaspoon salt
- ¼ teaspoon freshly ground pepper

Spray the grill rack with nonstick spray; prepare the grill for a medium-hot fire using the direct method (see page 81).

To make the glaze, combine the preserves, lemon juice, and crushed red pepper in a small bowl; set aside.

Sprinkle the duck with the coriander, salt, and pepper. Place on the grill rack and grill 3–4 minutes. Turn the duck over and brush with half of the glaze, then grill 3 minutes longer. Turn the duck again and brush with the remaining glaze and grill until cooked through about 1 minute longer.

PER SERVING (1 piece duck): 179 Cal, 1 g Fat, 0 g Sat Fat, 0 g Trans Fat, 83 mg Chol, 502 mg Sod, 11 g Carb, 0 g Fib, 29 g Prot, 22 mg Calc. *POINTS* value: *4.*

Duck with Sweet-and-Sour Cabbage

Cooking the cabbage takes a while, but it is well worthwhile—you can do it up to 5 days ahead, store it in the refrigerator, and reheat in a saucepan. Wood chips sprinkled on the grill give a wonderfully smoky flavor to the duck.

MAKES 4 SERVINGS

4 cups shredded red cabbage
1 cup thinly sliced red onions
2 small apples, peeled, cored, and diced

1 cup cranberry juice cocktail
½ cup red-wine vinegar
4 (5–6-ounce) skinless boneless duck breasts

Combine the cabbage, onions, apples, cranberry juice, and vinegar in a large saucepan; cook, covered, over low heat until well softened, about 2 hours, stirring every half hour or so.

Spray the grill rack with nonstick spray; prepare the grill for a medium-hot fire using the direct method (see page 81).

Soak ½ cup hickory, oak, or cherry wood chips in water for 15 minutes; drain, and sprinkle them over the hot coals.

Place the duck breasts on the grill rack, and grill, covered, until cooked through, about 3 minutes on each side. Serve the duck with the cabbage.

PER SERVING (1 piece duck with ½ cup cabbage): 248 Cal, 3 g Fat, 1 g Sat Fat, 0 g Trans Fat, 162 mg Chol, 137 mg Sod, 22 g Carb, 3 g Fib, 33 g Prot, 54 mg Calc. *POINTS* value: *5.*

TIP This recipe calls for hickory, oak, or cherry wood chips, but you might consider other woods such as apple, cherry, maple, or peach—all of which would flavor the duck beautifully.

Herb-Marinated Quails

Wine, garlic, and herbs combine to make a subtle marinade for these little birds that become crisp and delicious when grilled. Be careful not to overcook them—they make for speedy grilling. You'll get about 1½ ounces of cooked meat from each quail.

MAKES 4 SERVINGS

8 (¼-pound) quails
½ cup dry red or
    white wine
1 tablespoon + 1 teaspoon
    olive oil
1 large garlic clove, minced

½ teaspoon dried thyme leaves,
    crumbled
½ teaspoon dried rosemary
    leaves, crumbled
½ teaspoon coarsely ground
    black pepper

Cut the quails up the back; open and flatten them with the heel of your hand. Combine the wine, oil, garlic, thyme, rosemary, and pepper in a large dish. Add the quails, turning to coat; marinate for 10 minutes at room temperature, or cover and marinate in the refrigerator for up to 2 hours.

Spray the grill rack with nonstick spray; prepare the grill for a hot fire using the direct method (see page 81).

Place the quails on the grill rack, skin-side up, and grill for 3 minutes; turn and grill until crisp and brown and the juices run clear when pierced with a fork, 4–5 minutes longer.

Transfer 2 quails to each of 4 plates and serve them hot or at room temperature. Remove the skin before eating.

PER SERVING (2 quails): 206 Cal, 9 g Fat, 2 g Sat Fat, 0 g Trans Fat, 0 mg Chol, 56 mg Sod, 1 g Carb, 0 g Fib, 23 g Prot, 24 mg Calc. **POINTS** value: **5.**

TIP Although a chef's knife works well for cutting up quail, poultry shears make the task a breeze.

Delicious Fish and Shellfish

Spicy Salmon Steaks with Tarragon Sauce

Salmon is so delicious cooked on a grill it will even convert those who ordinarily turn up their noses at fish. The mustard marinade provides a sharp counterpoint to the richness of the fish. Any leftovers can be made into a spectacular salmon salad. Simply mash the salmon and sauce together and add a few drained capers, minced celery, and a little more reduced-calorie mayonnaise.

MAKES 4 SERVINGS

¼ cup dry white wine

¼ cup white-wine vinegar

1 garlic clove, peeled and bruised

3 tablespoons Dijon mustard

2 tablespoons fresh lemon juice

½ teaspoon coarsely ground black pepper

4 (4-ounce) salmon steaks, about 1 inch thick

2 tablespoons + 2 teaspoons reduced-calorie mayonnaise

1–2 tablespoons minced fresh tarragon, to taste

Combine the wine, vinegar, and garlic in a small saucepan. Boil over high heat until the liquid is reduced by half. Discard the garlic; whisk in the mustard, lemon juice, and pepper. Set 1 tablespoon aside.

Let the remaining wine mixture cool, then place in a zip-close plastic bag; add the salmon steaks. Squeeze out the air and seal the bag; turn to coat the salmon. Let the salmon marinate for 10 minutes in the sauce.

Spray the grill rack with nonstick spray; prepare the grill for a medium fire using the direct method (see page 81).

To make the tarragon sauce, whisk together the reserved 1 tablespoon wine mixture, the mayonnaise, and tarragon in a small bowl; set aside.

Remove the salmon from the marinade; discard the marinade. Place the salmon steaks on the grill rack and grill until just opaque in the center, about 5 minutes on each side. Serve the salmon with the tarragon sauce.

PER SERVING (1 salmon steak and 1 tablespoon sauce): 208 Cal, 10 g Fat, 2 g Sat Fat, 0 g Trans Fat, 66 mg Chol, 378 mg Sod, 3 g Carb, 0 g Fib, 23 g Prot, 27 mg Calc. *POINTS* value: *5.*

GRILLED TUNA WITH CORN AND PEA SAUTÉ

Grilled Tuna with Corn and Pea Sauté

Meaty tuna steaks are topped with a citrus-cilantro mayonnaise and served with colorful sautéed veggies. The addition of grilled red onion gives the vegetables a smoky flavor and a touch of sweetness.

MAKES 4 SERVINGS

¼ cup fat-free mayonnaise

1 tablespoon chopped fresh cilantro

1 teaspoon fresh lime juice

4 (¼-inch-thick) slices red onion

4 teaspoons extra-virgin olive oil

2 garlic cloves, minced

1 (10-ounce) package frozen corn kernels

1 cup frozen peas

½ avocado, pitted, peeled, and diced

1 teaspoon salt

¼ teaspoon freshly ground pepper

4 (6-ounce) tuna steaks, about ¾ inch thick

Combine the mayonnaise, cilantro, and lime juice in a small bowl; set aside.

Spray the grill rack with nonstick spray; prepare the grill for a medium-hot fire using the direct method (see page 81).

Brush the onion slices with 1 teaspoon of the oil and place on the grill rack. Grill the onion 5–6 minutes. Turn and grill until tender, 5–6 minutes longer. Transfer to a cutting board and coarsely chop.

Heat 2 teaspoons of the oil in a large nonstick skillet over medium-high heat. Add the garlic and cook, stirring constantly, until fragrant, about 30 seconds. Add the corn and cook, stirring occasionally, until lightly browned, about 7 minutes. Add the peas and cook, stirring occasionally, until hot, about 3 minutes. Remove the skillet from the heat. Stir in the grilled onions, the avocado, ½ teaspoon of the salt, and ⅛ teaspoon of the pepper. Cover and keep warm.

Brush the tuna with the remaining 1 teaspoon oil and sprinkle with the remaining ½ teaspoon salt and ⅛ teaspoon pepper. Place the tuna on the grill rack and grill until done to taste, 4–5 minutes on each side for medium. Serve with the corn and pea sauté and the cilantro mayonnaise.

PER SERVING (1 tuna steak, about ⅔ cup corn and pea sauté, and 1 generous tablespoon cilantro mayonnaise): 377 Cal, 11 g Fat, 2 g Sat Fat, 0 g Trans Fat, 76 mg Chol, 807 mg Sod, 28 g Carb, 6 g Fib, 43 g Prot, 53 mg Calc. *POINTS* value: *8.*

Asian Tuna with Water Chestnuts on a Stick

Garlic, ginger, and honey are the fabulous flavors that shine through in these easy-to-make kebabs. You can prepare the marinade up to a day ahead and store it in the refrigerator until you are ready to use it.

MAKES 4 SERVINGS

¼ cup reduced-sodium soy sauce
2 tablespoons rice-wine vinegar
2 tablespoons dry sherry
6 garlic cloves, minced
1 tablespoon minced peeled fresh ginger

2 teaspoons honey
¼ teaspoon freshly ground pepper
16 whole canned water chestnuts, drained
2 (10-ounce) tuna steaks, about ¾-inch thick

Spray the grill rack with nonstick spray; prepare the grill for a medium fire using the direct method (see page 81). If using wooden skewers, soak them in water for 30 minutes.

To make the marinade, combine the soy sauce, vinegar, sherry, garlic, ginger, honey, and pepper in a small bowl.

Thread 4 water chestnuts onto each of 4 (6-inch) metal or wooden skewers, spacing them ⅛ inch apart. Brush the water chestnuts with about one-third of the marinade, and place them on the grill rack. Grill, turning the skewers occasionally, until the water chestnuts are lightly browned and heated through, about 5 minutes.

Meanwhile, brush the tuna steaks with the remaining two-thirds marinade and place them on the grill rack. Grill the tuna until done to taste, 4–5 minutes on each side for medium.

Transfer the tuna steaks to a cutting board, and cut them into ⅛-inch-thick slices. Divide the tuna evenly among 4 plates, and top each with a skewer of water chestnuts.

PER SERVING (½ tuna steak and 4 water chestnuts): 269 Cal, 7 g Fat, 2 g Sat Fat, 0 g Trans Fat, 54 mg Chol, 660 mg Sod, 11 g Carb, 0 g Fib, 35 g Prot, 12 mg Calc. *POINTS* value: *6.*

Swordfish Kebabs with Spicy Nut Sauce

Swordfish is ideal for grilling because it doesn't fall apart easily, doesn't tend to stick to the grill, and is always beautifully enhanced by a marinade or sauce.

MAKES 4 SERVINGS

¼ cup low-sodium chicken broth

2 tablespoons fresh lemon juice

1 tablespoon minced fresh dill

2 teaspoons Dijon mustard

½ teaspoon salt

½ teaspoon freshly ground pepper

1 pound swordfish, cut into
   1-inch chunks

1 zucchini, cut into
   1-inch chunks

1 red bell pepper, seeded and
   cut into ½-inch pieces

12 cherry tomatoes

¼ cup coarsely chopped walnuts

1 tablespoon chopped onion

2 teaspoons olive oil

Combine the broth, lemon juice, dill, mustard, ¼ teaspoon of the salt, and ¼ teaspoon of the pepper in a zip-close plastic bag; add the swordfish. Squeeze out the air and seal the bag; turn to coat the fish. Refrigerate, turning the bag occasionally, at least 1 hour or overnight.

Pour the marinade into a small saucepan, and boil, stirring constantly, 3 minutes. Add water, if necessary, to keep the amount of liquid at about ¼ cup.

Spray the grill rack with nonstick spray; prepare the grill for a medium fire using the direct method (see page 81). If using wooden skewers, soak them in water for 30 minutes. Preheat the oven to 350°F. Spray a baking sheet with nonstick spray.

Thread the fish, zucchini, bell pepper, and tomatoes alternately onto 12 (12-inch) metal or wooden skewers. Sprinkle with remaining ¼ teaspoon salt and ¼ teaspoon pepper.

Place the kebabs on the grill rack and grill 4 minutes on each side. Transfer the kebabs to the baking sheet and bake until the fish is just opaque and the vegetables are cooked through, about 5 minutes.

Meanwhile, combine the cooked marinade with the walnuts in a food processor; pulse several times until the walnuts are finely chopped. Add the onion and oil; pulse for 30 seconds more. Serve the kebabs with the sauce.

PER SERVING (3 kebabs): 231 Cal, 12 g Fat, 2 g Sat Fat, 0 g Trans Fat, 41 mg Chol, 495 mg Sod, 8 g Carb, 2 g Fib, 24 g Prot, 31 mg Calc. **POINTS** value: **5.**

Lime-Tamari Grilled Swordfish

This piquant Tex-Mex marinade adds zest to swordfish steaks, but it also works well with most white fish. Try it with sea bass, mahi mahi, grouper, or tilefish.

MAKES 4 SERVINGS

¼ cup dry vermouth

2 tablespoons fresh lime juice

1 tablespoon minced fresh cilantro

1 tablespoon extra-virgin olive oil

1 tablespoon light tamari or reduced-sodium soy sauce

⅛ teaspoon mixed herb-seasoned salt

4 (5-ounce) swordfish steaks, 1 inch thick

Spray the grill rack with nonstick spray; prepare the grill for a medium fire using the direct method (see page 81).

Combine the vermouth, lime juice, cilantro, oil, tamari, and seasoned salt in a zip-close plastic bag; add the swordfish steaks. Squeeze out the air and seal the bag; turn to coat the fish. Refrigerate, turning the bag occasionally, about 1 hour.

Pour the marinade into a small saucepan and boil, stirring constantly, 3 minutes. Add water, if necessary, to keep the amount of liquid at about ¼ cup.

Place the swordfish steaks on the grill rack and grill until the fish is just opaque in the center, about 4 minutes on each side.

Place the fish on a serving platter; spoon the cooked marinade over the fish.

PER SERVING (1 swordfish steak and 1 tablespoon marinade): 225 Cal, 9 g Fat, 2 g Sat Fat, 0 g Trans Fat, 55 mg Chol, 349 mg Sod, 2 g Carb, 0 g Fib, 29 g Prot, 9 mg Calc. *POINTS* value: *5.*

Red Snapper with Corn-Raisin Relish

The relish is sweetened with pineapple, giving this dish a tropical taste, perfect on a hot summer night. If you can't find red snapper, substitute swordfish, cod, tilefish, or any other white saltwater fish.

MAKES 4 SERVINGS

1 cup cider vinegar

2 tablespoons sugar

2 cups fresh or thawed frozen corn kernels

1 cup thinly sliced red onions

¼ cup + 2 tablespoons raisins

¼ teaspoon cinnamon

¼ teaspoon ground cloves

½ cup drained canned crushed pineapple with 2 tablespoons juice

4 (5-ounce) red snapper fillets, patted dry

To make the relish, combine the vinegar and sugar in a medium saucepan; bring to a boil, stirring constantly to dissolve the sugar. Reduce the heat; stir in the corn, onions, raisins, cinnamon, and cloves. Simmer, uncovered, stirring frequently until the liquid is reduced slightly, about 20 minutes. Add the pineapple and 2 tablespoons juice, increase the heat to high, and cook, stirring frequently, until the relish is thickened and syrupy, about 10 minutes longer.

Meanwhile, spray the grill rack with nonstick spray; prepare the grill for a medium fire using the direct method (see page 81).

Place the red snapper on the grill rack and grill until just opaque in the center, 2–3 minutes on each side. Serve with the relish.

PER SERVING (1 snapper fillet and ½ cup relish): 322 Cal, 3 g Fat, 1 g Sat Fat, 0 g Trans Fat, 52 mg Chol, 110 mg Sod, 45 g Carb, 4 g Fib, 33 g Prot, 77 mg Calc. *POINTS* value: **6.**

TIP Try using a wide (about 5-inch) slotted spatula when you are grilling fish. It will make turning the fish and transferring it to serving plates easy.

Snapper Fillets with Summer Vegetables

This is a quick-and-easy, low-fat way to grill fish. Experiment with different kinds of fish (flounder, grouper, sea bass) and various vegetable combinations (onions, cucumbers, beets, turnips, parsnips, or tomatoes).

MAKES 4 SERVINGS

- 4 **(5-ounce) red snapper fillets**
- ½ **teaspoon salt**
- ¼ **teaspoon freshly ground pepper**
- 1 **medium zucchini, cut into thin strips**
- 1 **medium yellow squash, cut into thin strips**

- ½ **small leek, cut into thin strips**
- 1 **medium carrot, cut into thin strips**
- 4 **tablespoons bottled clam juice, or fish or vegetable broth**
- 4 **lemon slices**

Prepare the grill for a medium fire using the direct method (see page 81).

Lightly spray 4 (18-inch) squares of foil with nonstick spray. Place 1 fish fillet in the center of each foil square and season each with one-fourth of the salt and pepper; distribute one-fourth each of the zucchini, squash, leek, and carrot evenly over each fillet. Top each with 1 tablespoon of the clam juice and 1 lemon slice.

Make the packets by bringing 2 sides of the foil up to meet in the center and pressing the edges together to seal. Then fold the edges of each end together to seal. Allowing room for the packets to expand, crimp the edges together to seal.

Place the packets on the grill rack and grill for 10 minutes. The packets will puff up as the fish and vegetables cook. Remove the packets from the grill and open them carefully, avoiding the steam. Transfer the contents of each packet to plates and serve at once.

PER SERVING (1 snapper fillet and 1½ cups vegetables): 170 Cal, 2 g Fat, 0 g Sat Fat, 0 g Trans Fat, 50 mg Chol, 399 mg Sod, 8 g Carb, 2 g Fib, 30 g Prot, 73 mg Calc. *POINTS* value: *3.*

SNAPPER FILLETS WITH
SUMMER VEGETABLES

 Indian-Style Cod

Exotic spices in this colorful dish provide a tangy twist to an otherwise mild fish. Marinate the cod overnight for the fullest flavor. Be aware that cod is relatively delicate and tends to stick to the grill, even if it has been oiled. Serve with Pita Breads with Thyme (page 188), if you like and deduct it from your **weekly *POINTS* Allowance.**

MAKES 4 SERVINGS

¼ cup yogurt cheese (see TIP below)

¼ cup fresh lime juice

1 garlic clove

1 (1-inch) piece peeled fresh ginger

1 tablespoon curry powder

¼ teaspoon cinnamon

¼ teaspoon ground cumin

¼ teaspoon ground cayenne

⅛ teaspoon ground cloves

4 (5-ounce) cod steaks

Combine the yogurt cheese, lime juice, garlic, ginger, curry, cinnamon, cumin, cayenne, and cloves in a blender or food processor; puree until smooth. Pour the marinade into a zip-close plastic bag; add the cod steaks. Squeeze out the air and seal the bag; turn to coat the cod. Refrigerate, turning the bag occasionally, at least 1 hour, or, ideally, overnight.

Prepare the grill for a medium fire using the direct method (see page 81). Spray a grill basket with nonstick spray.

Remove the fish from the marinade; pour the marinade into a small saucepan and boil, stirring constantly, 3 minutes. Add water, if necessary, to keep the amount of liquid at about ⅓ cup.

Place the fish in the grill basket and baste with the marinade. Grill the fish, turning once and basting with the remaining marinade, until the cod is just opaque in the center, about 3 minutes on each side.

Carefully remove the cod from the grill basket and serve at once.

PER SERVING (1 cod steak): 138 Cal, 1 g Fat, 0 g Sat Fat, 0 g Trans Fat, 61 mg Chol, 88 mg Sod, 4 g Carb, 1 g Fib, 27 g Prot, 71 mg Calc. *POINTS* value: *3.*

TIP To make yogurt cheese, place ½ cup plain fat-free yogurt in a sieve lined with a damp paper towel over a bowl. Refrigerate, covered, 1½ hours or overnight. Discard the liquid in the bowl. Makes ¼ cup yogurt cheese.

 Cod Steaks Grilled in Grape Leaves

Not only do grape leaves eliminate the problem of fish sticking to the grill, they are also edible and quite tasty. The packets can be prepared in the morning and refrigerated until grilling time. These cod-filled grape leaves are delicious cold, so you might want to grill a few extras.

MAKES 4 SERVINGS

16 grape leaves (see TIP below)

4 (5-ounce) boneless cod steaks (about 1 inch thick)

8 paper-thin lemon slices

½ teaspoon dried oregano

½ teaspoon freshly ground pepper

4 teaspoons olive oil

Bring 2 quarts of water to a rolling boil in a tea kettle or a saucepan. Place the grape leaves in a colander in the sink; pour boiling water over them. Rinse with cold water at once and drain.

Soak about 8 feet of kitchen twine in water.

Place about 3 grape leaves, overlapping each other by half, on a work surface. Place a cod steak in the center of the leaves. Top the cod steak with 2 lemon slices, a pinch each of oregano and pepper, and 1 teaspoon of oil. Wrap the fish in the leaves (use additional leaves, if needed, to enclose the fish completely) and tie crosswise and lengthwise with the twine, as you would tie a small package. Repeat to make a total of 4 packets. Cover the packets with foil, and refrigerate until ready to grill.

Spray the grill rack with nonstick spray; prepare the grill for a medium fire using the direct method (see page 81).

Place the packets directly on the grill rack and grill, turning them often to avoid charring the leaves, about 10 minutes. Transfer the packets to warm plates, remove the twine, and serve at once.

PER SERVING (1 packet): 179 Cal, 5 g Fat, 1 g Sat Fat, 0 g Trans Fat, 61 mg Chol, 877 mg Sod, 1 g Carb, 0 g Fib, 25 g Prot, 111 mg Calc. *POINTS* value: *4.*

TIP Grape leaves are available in most supermarkets, in jars or cans, often preserved in brine. We recommend rinsing them before using. Grape leaves, often stuffed with rice and meat, are popular in Greece and the Middle East.

Easy Asian-Marinated Halibut

This spicy-sweet treatment complements lightly flavored halibut beautifully. If halibut is unavailable, you can substitute snapper, cod, or any other firm, white-fleshed fish.

MAKES 6 SERVINGS

¼ cup honey

2 tablespoons reduced-sodium soy sauce

2 tablespoons fresh lemon juice

1 tablespoon Asian (dark) sesame oil

2 garlic cloves, minced

1 teaspoon ground ginger

½ teaspoon dry mustard

½ teaspoon crushed red pepper

½ teaspoon freshly ground pepper

6 (½-pound) halibut steaks

Combine the honey, soy sauce, lemon juice, oil, garlic, ginger, mustard, crushed red pepper, and ground pepper in a zip-close plastic bag; add the halibut. Squeeze out the air and seal the bag; turn to coat the halibut. Refrigerate, turning the bag occasionally, about 1 hour.

Spray the grill rack with nonstick spray; prepare the grill for a medium fire using the direct method (see page 81).

Remove the fish from the marinade. Pour the marinade into a small saucepan and boil, stirring constantly, 3 minutes. Add water, if necessary, to keep the amount of liquid at about ⅓ cup.

Place the halibut steaks on the grill rack and grill, brushing occasionally with the marinade, until just opaque in the center, 4–5 minutes on each side.

PER SERVING (1 halibut steak): 310 Cal, 7 g Fat, 1 g Sat Fat, 0 g Trans Fat, 70 mg Chol, 318 mg Sod, 13 g Carb, 0 g Fib, 49 g Prot, 108 mg Calc. **POINTS** value: **7.**

TIP Asian (dark) sesame oil is available in Asian markets, specialty food stores, and many supermarkets. It adds an intense sesame flavor, which is integral to this dish. You can substitute regular sesame oil or vegetable oil, but the flavor will be very different.

Thyme-Seasoned Grouper

A firm and almost sweet white-fleshed fish, grouper cooks beautifully on the grill, but use a grill basket, sprayed with nonstick spray, for extra insurance against sticking. Serve with Spicy Potato Wedges (page 142) and Minted Green Beans (page 130) for a hearty, yet nutritious, supper.

MAKES 4 SERVINGS

2 tablespoons dry white wine

1 tablespoon white-wine vinegar

1 tablespoon olive oil

2 garlic cloves, minced

1 teaspoon tomato paste

½ teaspoon dried thyme leaves

¼ teaspoon freshly ground pepper

4 (5-ounce) grouper steaks, about 1 inch thick

Combine the wine, vinegar, oil, garlic, tomato paste, thyme, and pepper in a zip-close plastic bag; add the grouper. Squeeze out the air and seal the bag; turn to coat the fish. Let stand for 10 minutes.

Prepare the grill for a medium fire using the direct method (see page 81). Spray a grill basket with nonstick spray.

Place the fish in the grill basket; place the basket on the grill rack. Grill the fish until just opaque in the center, about 5 minutes on each side.

PER SERVING (1 grouper steak): 164 Cal, 5 g Fat, 1 g Sat Fat, 0 g Trans Fat, 52 mg Chol, 87 mg Sod, 1 g Carb, 0 g Fib, 28 g Prot, 45 mg Calc. **POINTS** value: **4.**

Quick-Grilled Bluefish Fillets

Fresh lime juice, coriander, and oregano combine to make a robust southwestern seasoning, which works best with a fish that has a lot of flavor, such as bluefish. If bluefish is unavailable, you can substitute swordfish or tuna.

MAKES 4 SERVINGS

2 tablespoons fresh lime juice
½ teaspoon ground coriander
½ teaspoon dried oregano

½ teaspoon freshly ground pepper
4 (½-pound) bluefish fillets
(about ¾ inch thick)

Spray the grill rack with nonstick spray; prepare the grill for a hot fire using the direct method (see page 81).

Combine the lime juice, coriander, oregano, and pepper in a zip-close plastic bag; add the bluefish. Squeeze out the air and seal the bag; turn to coat the fish. Let stand about 5 minutes. Remove the fish and discard the marinade.

Place the bluefish on the grill rack and grill until just opaque in the center, about 3 minutes on each side.

PER SERVING (1 bluefish fillet): 285 Cal, 10 g Fat, 2 g Sat Fat, 0 g Trans Fat, 134 mg Chol, 136 mg Sod, 1 g Carb, 0 g Fib, 46 g Prot, 21 mg Calc. *POINTS* value: *7.*

Shrimp with Sweet Ginger Sauce

Scallions, soy sauce, fresh ginger, garlic, lemon, and brown sugar are some of the delicious flavors of Japan that combine to marinate shrimp for grilling as well as to make a delicious dipping sauce to serve alongside.

MAKES 4 SERVINGS

¼ cup chopped scallions

2 tablespoons reduced-sodium soy sauce

1 tablespoon minced peeled fresh ginger

3 garlic cloves, minced

1 tablespoon fresh lemon juice

2 teaspoons packed brown sugar

1¼ pounds large shrimp, peeled and deveined

Combine the scallions, soy sauce, ginger, garlic, lemon juice, and sugar in a zip-close plastic bag; add the shrimp. Squeeze out the air and seal the bag; turn to coat the shrimp. Refrigerate, turning the bag occasionally, about 2 hours.

Spray the grill rack with nonstick spray; prepare the grill for a medium fire using the direct method (see page 81). Spray a grill basket with nonstick spray.

Remove the shrimp from the marinade. Pour the marinade into a small saucepan and boil, stirring constantly, 3 minutes. Add water, if necessary, to keep the amount of liquid at about ¼ cup. Let the mixture cool and pour it into a small serving bowl to serve as a dipping sauce.

Place the shrimp in the grill basket; place the grill basket on the grill rack. Grill the shrimp until just opaque in the center, 2–3 minutes on each side. Serve the shrimp with the sauce.

PER SERVING (¼ of shrimp and 1 tablespoon sauce): 131 Cal, 1 g Fat, 0 g Sat Fat, 0 g Trans Fat, 210 mg Chol, 547 mg Sod, 5 g Carb, 0 g Fib, 24 g Prot, 57 mg Calc. **POINTS** value: **3.**

SPICY SHRIMP WITH PAPAYA SALSA

Spicy Shrimp with Papaya Salsa

You'll love the spicy, south-of-the-border flavors of this shrimp dish, which looks—and tastes—spectacular with colorful, sweet papaya salsa. You might like to try it with Marinated Belgian Endive (page 122).

MAKES 4 SERVINGS

1½ teaspoons paprika

½ teaspoon dried thyme leaves

½ teaspoon salt

½ teaspoon freshly ground pepper

⅛–¼ teaspoon cayenne

1¼ pounds large shrimp, peeled and deveined

2 cups cubed papaya

¼ cup chopped scallions

2 tablespoons fresh lime juice

Prepare the grill for a hot fire using the direct method (see page 81). Spray a grill basket with nonstick spray.

Combine the paprika, thyme, salt, pepper, and cayenne in a medium bowl. Add the shrimp and toss to coat.

Meanwhile, to make the salsa, combine the papaya, scallions, and lime juice in a bowl; set aside.

Place the shrimp in the grill basket; place the grill basket on the grill rack. Grill the shrimp until just opaque in the center, 2–3 minutes on each side. Serve the shrimp with the salsa.

PER SERVING (¼ of shrimp and ½ cup salsa): 150 Cal, 1 g Fat, 0 g Sat Fat, 0 g Trans Fat, 221 mg Chol, 531 mg Sod, 10 g Carb, 1 g Fib, 25 g Prot, 79 mg Calc. **POINTS** value: **3.**

Speedy Pesto Scallops

This unusual pesto of parsley, goat cheese, and walnuts, spiked with a little brandy is intensely flavored, so we make just enough to coat the scallops. Try these tasty tidbits with Warm Radicchio with Basil Dressing (page 155) and Grill-Roasted Garlic Mashed Potatoes (page 143).

MAKES 4 SERVINGS ○

¾ cup minced flat-leaf parsley

2 tablespoons crumbled goat cheese

1 tablespoon brandy

2 tablespoons finely chopped walnuts

1 tablespoon fresh lemon juice

1 tablespoon olive oil

1 garlic clove, minced

1¼ pounds sea scallops

Prepare the grill for a hot fire using the direct method (see page 81). Spray a grill basket with nonstick spray.

To make the pesto, combine the parsley, cheese, brandy, walnuts, lemon juice, oil, and garlic in a blender or food processor; puree until smooth.

Transfer the pesto to a medium bowl; add the scallops and toss to coat.

Place the scallops in the grill basket; place the grill basket on the grill rack. Grill until just opaque in the center, about 2 minutes on each side. Serve at once.

PER SERVING (¼ of scallops): 193 Cal, 7 g Fat, 1 g Sat Fat, 0 g Trans Fat, 50 mg Chol, 251 mg Sod, 5 g Carb, 1 g Fib, 25 g Prot, 61 mg Calc. *POINTS* value: *4.*

Grilled Calamari with Mustard Dressing

We grill calamari (squid) unadorned until it is lightly charred, then toss it, while still warm, with delicious mustard vinaigrette. It's quick, easy, and very tasty. If you prefer, you can marinate the squid briefly in the dressing before cooking, then grill, basting once or twice with the dressing.

MAKES 4 SERVINGS

2 tablespoons fresh lemon juice	¼ teaspoon crushed red pepper
2 tablespoons red-wine vinegar	1 tablespoon + 1 teaspoon olive oil
2 teaspoons Dijon mustard	
½ teaspoon dried thyme leaves	1¼ pounds cleaned small squid
½ teaspoon salt	4 lemon wedges, for garnish

Prepare the grill for a hot fire using the direct method (see page 81). Spray a grill basket with nonstick spray.

To make the dressing, combine the lemon juice, vinegar, mustard, thyme, salt, and crushed red pepper in a medium bowl; whisk in the oil a little at a time. Set aside for the flavors to develop, about 10 minutes.

Place the calamari in the grill basket. Place the grill basket on the grill rack and grill, turning frequently, until golden and lightly charred, about 8 minutes.

Slice the calamari into ½-inch pieces, add to the dressing in the bowl, and toss well to coat. Serve, garnished with the lemon wedges.

PER SERVING (1 cup sliced squid): 176 Cal, 6 g Fat, 1 g Sat Fat, 0 g Trans Fat, 331 mg Chol, 398 mg Sod, 5 g Carb, 0 g Fib, 22 g Prot, 52 mg Calc. *POINTS* value: *4.*

TIP Although you can clean squid yourself, you will quickly discover that it is rather time consuming and tedious. It's much easier to buy it cleaned or ask your fishmonger to do it for you.

Oysters with Shallot Sauce

True oyster lovers need no side dishes to accompany this heavenly fare, but you might precede the feast with Creamy Corn Chowder (page 22) to placate extra-hungry guests.

MAKES 4 SERVINGS

½ cup dry white vermouth
1 teaspoon or more freshly cracked black pepper
½ cup white-wine vinegar
1 tablespoon minced shallot or scallion

4 dozen medium oysters, scrubbed and rinsed well
Hot pepper sauce, to taste
Lemon wedges, for garnish

Spray the grill rack with nonstick spray; prepare the grill for a medium fire using the direct method (see page 81).

To make the shallot sauce, heat the vermouth to a simmer in a small saucepan. Add the pepper; remove the saucepan from the heat, and stir in the vinegar and shallot. Let stand until the mixture is cool.

Place the oysters on the grill rack. Grill the oysters, flat-side up, until they open, about 4 minutes. Discard any that do not open after 5 minutes. Using an oven mitt to hold the oyster, pry off the top shell with an oyster knife or the rounded end of a "church key"-type bottle opener. Divide the oysters evenly among 4 plates and serve with the shallot sauce, hot pepper sauce, and lemon wedges.

PER SERVING (12 oysters and ¼ cup shallot sauce): 116 Cal, 3 g Fat, 1 g Sat Fat, 0 g Trans Fat, 62 mg Chol, 129 mg Sod, 6 g Carb, 0 g Fib, 8 g Prot, 57 mg Calc. *POINTS* value: *3.*

TIP Live oysters should always be as fresh as possible, so be sure to buy from a place you trust, with a large turnover. Also, cook oysters soon after buying. Store them in the refrigerator, covered with a damp towel, for no more than 2 days. Scrub them well under cool water before grilling. Discard any oysters that are not tightly closed or that have broken shells.

Lobster with Dilled Yogurt Sauce

Scandinavian flavors of dill and lemon serve this simple grilled lobster very well. Lobster needs to be very fresh, so buy it just before you're ready to cook it, and have the fishmonger split and clean it for you.

MAKES 4 SERVINGS

- ¾ cup yogurt cheese (see TIP below)
- 2 tablespoons minced fresh dill
- 2 tablespoons fresh lemon juice
- ⅜ teaspoon freshly ground pepper
- 2 (1½-pound) lobsters, split and cleaned
- ¼ teaspoon salt
- 4 lemon slices, for garnish

Spray the grill rack with nonstick spray; prepare the grill for a medium fire using the direct method (see page 81).

To make the yogurt sauce, combine the yogurt cheese, dill, lemon juice, and ¼ teaspoon of the pepper in a medium bowl; stir to blend. Set aside.

Season the lobsters with the salt and remaining ⅛ teaspoon pepper. Break the lobster claws off and crack them with the back of a heavy knife. Place the lobsters on the grill rack, split-side down; place the claws on a slightly cooler part of the grill and cover them loosely with foil. Grill the lobsters and claws until the meat is just opaque in the center, about 9 minutes.

Remove the lobsters from the grill and separate the halves. Remove the claws and crack through completely. Place half a lobster and 1 claw on each plate. Garnish each plate with a lemon slice and serve with the yogurt sauce.

PER SERVING (½ lobster, 1 claw, and 3 tablespoons yogurt sauce): 117 Cal, 1 g Fat, 0 g Sat Fat, 0 g Trans Fat, 61 mg Chol, 491 mg Sod, 5 g Carb, 0 g Fib, 21 g Prot, 170 mg Calc. **POINTS** value: **2.**

TIP To make yogurt cheese, place 1½ cups plain fat-free yogurt in a sieve lined with a damp paper towel over a bowl. Refrigerate, covered with plastic wrap, about 1½ hours or overnight. Discard liquid in bowl. Makes ¾ cup yogurt cheese.

Vegetables on
the Side

✓ Grilled Corn on the Cob

There's nothing so basic to summer grilling as deliciously charred, fresh corn on the cob. The corn can be grilled in advance and used for a variety of dishes, including salsas, salads, soups, and chowders. Once you remove the kernels from the cob, you can cover and refrigerate them for up to 3 days or pack them in freezer bags and freeze for up to 3 months.

MAKES 8 SERVINGS 🥕

8 ears fresh corn, unhusked

Spray the grill rack with nonstick spray; prepare the grill for a medium fire using the direct method (see page 81).

Gently pull back the outer leaves of the corn husks without removing the leaves completely; remove the silk. Smooth the leaves back over the corn and soak in cold water, about 10 minutes.

Place the corn on the grill rack, cover the grill, and grill until the corn is cooked and lightly charred, 15–20 minutes.

Peel the husks from the corn, trim away the stems, and serve at once. Or, let the corn cool for a few minutes, then stand the cobs on end and cut the kernels from the cobs with a knife.

PER SERVING (1 ear or ½ cup kernels): 97 Cal, 1 g Fat, 0 g Sat Fat, 0 g Trans Fat, 0 mg Chol, 15 mg Sod, 23 g Carb, 4 g Fib, 3 g Prot, 2 mg Calc. **POINTS** value: *1.*

✓ Grilled Onion Slices

Perhaps the most popular vegetable topping for grilled burgers, these grilled onion slices also make a welcome addition to any summertime salad or sandwich. Try to use Bermuda, Spanish, or Vidalia onions; they are the sweetest and most succulent varieties. Grill some whenever you have room on the barbecue; they won't go to waste.

MAKES 8 SERVINGS 🥕

6 large red or white onions, cut into ½-inch-thick slices

Spray the grill rack with nonstick spray; prepare the grill for a medium-low fire using the direct method (see page 81).

Place the onions on the grill rack and grill, turning once with tongs, until cooked through, 10–12 minutes on each side.

PER SERVING (about 4 slices): 43 Cal, 0 g Fat, 0 g Sat Fat, 0 g Trans Fat, 0 mg Chol, 3 mg Sod, 10 g Carb, 2 g Fib, 1 g Prot, 23 mg Calc. *POINTS* value: *1.*

TIP A grill basket is helpful for holding the sliced onions together, but it is not necessary.

Garlicky Grilled Bell Peppers

Grill a big batch of these peppers to keep on hand for salads, sandwiches, and pasta dishes. They will keep for up to 5 days stored in containers in the refrigerator or up to 6 months stored in freezer bags in the freezer.

MAKES 16 SERVINGS

- 4 green bell peppers
- 4 red bell peppers
- 4 yellow bell peppers
- ¼ cup dry white wine
- 2 tablespoons + 2 teaspoons extra-virgin olive oil
- 2 tablespoons minced fresh basil (optional)
- 4–5 garlic cloves, slivered
- ½ teaspoon salt

Spray the grill rack with nonstick spray; prepare the grill for a hot fire using the direct method (see page 81).

Place the bell peppers on the grill rack and grill, turning as needed with tongs, until the skin is charred on all sides, 15–20 minutes. Place the bell peppers in a heavy paper bag or large covered bowl; let stand 20 minutes.

Working over a large bowl, carefully remove the charred skin, seeds, and stems from the bell peppers. Slice the bell peppers into strips; add the strips to the juices in the bowl. Add the wine, oil, basil (if using), garlic, and salt; toss to coat thoroughly. Serve at once or pack into containers and refrigerate or freeze.

PER SERVING (½ cup): 45 Cal, 2 g Fat, 0 g Sat Fat, 0 g Trans Fat, 0 mg Chol, 76 mg Sod, 6 g Carb, 1 g Fib, 1 g Prot, mg Calc. **POINTS** value: *1.*

TIP Bell peppers are a variety of sweet pepper. The red and yellow bell peppers are not another variety; they are merely green bell peppers that have ripened further, turning red then yellow. (Because they have been left on the vine longer, they are also a bit sweeter.) Orange, brown, and purple bell peppers are also available in many markets. For this recipe, use any color bell pepper that suits your fancy.

LEEKS WITH THYME-ORANGE
VINAIGRETTE

Leeks with Thyme-Orange Vinaigrette

Grilling brings out the natural sweetness of leeks while this zesty dressing adds subtle, but delicious, flavor. Serve with Marinated Flank Steak with Cherry Tomato Salad (page 35).

MAKES 4 SERVINGS

- 4 medium leeks
- 2 tablespoons minced fresh parsley
- 2 tablespoons white-wine vinegar
- 1 tablespoon olive oil
- 1 teaspoon water

- ½ teaspoon minced fresh thyme
- ½ teaspoon grated orange zest
- ½ teaspoon Dijon mustard
- ½ teaspoon salt
- ⅛ teaspoon freshly ground pepper

Spray the grill rack with nonstick spray; prepare the grill for a medium fire using the direct method (see page 81).

Trim away most of the dark green tops and the roots from the leeks, leaving the root ends intact to hold the layers together. Slice the leeks lengthwise to within a half inch of the root end. Hold the leeks by the root ends, fan open the layers, and rinse thoroughly under cold running water. Place the leeks in a large saucepan, cover with 2 inches of cold water, and bring to a boil. Cover the pan, reduce the heat, and simmer until the leeks are tender, about 5 minutes. Rinse the leeks in a colander under cold running water and drain on paper towels. Finish cutting through the leeks, lengthwise.

To make the vinaigrette, combine the parsley, vinegar, oil, water, thyme, orange zest, mustard, salt, and pepper in a small bowl; set aside.

Place the leeks on the grill rack and grill, turning once with tongs, until the leeks are lightly browned, 4–5 minutes on each side. Transfer 2 leek halves to each of 4 plates and drizzle evenly with the vinaigrette.

PER SERVING (2 leek halves and 1 tablespoon vinaigrette): 93 Cal, 4 g Fat, 0 g Sat Fat, 0 g Trans Fat, 0 mg Chol, 171 mg Sod, 15 g Carb, 1 g Fib, 2 g Prot, 64 mg Calc. **POINTS** value: **2.**

TIP Sand and dirt can get caught in the tightly wrapped leek leaves, so be sure to wash them thoroughly before using.

☑ Marinated Belgian Endive

Grilling is a marvelous way to cook this slightly bitter vegetable. It can be prepared and marinated ahead and grilled quickly at the last minute; be careful not to over char the delicate leaves.

MAKES 4 SERVINGS 🥕

2 tablespoons fresh lemon juice
1 tablespoon olive oil
Pinch freshly ground pepper

4 heads Belgian endive,
   halved lengthwise

Spray the grill rack with nonstick spray; prepare the grill for a medium fire using the direct method (see page 81).

Combine the lemon juice, oil, and pepper in a zip-close plastic bag; add the endive. Squeeze out the air and seal the bag; turn to coat the endive. Refrigerate, turning the bag occasionally, 1–2 hours.

Transfer the endive from the marinade to a plate. Reserve any remaining marinade. Place the endive along the edges of the grill rack and grill until cooked through but not charred, about 3 minutes on each side. Transfer the endive to a serving platter and drizzle with the marinade.

PER SERVING (2 endive halves): 47 Cal, 3 g Fat, 0 g Sat Fat, 0 g Trans Fat, 0 mg Chol, 9 mg Sod, 4 g Carb, 2 g Fib, 1 g Prot, 1 mg Calc. **POINTS** value: *1.*

Grilled Whole Tomatoes

Firm, vine-ripened summer tomatoes are sheer heaven cooked on the grill.
To help them hold their shape during the grilling process, be sure to use
tomatoes that are still a little firm; not overripe and soft. Plum tomatoes are
a fine alternative to beefsteak tomatoes.

MAKES 4 SERVINGS

- 4 garlic cloves, minced
- 1 tablespoon minced fresh basil
  or 1 teaspoon dried basil,
  oregano, or thyme
- 1 tablespoon olive oil
- Pinch salt
- 4 beefsteak tomatoes or 8 large
  plum tomatoes

Combine the garlic, basil, oil, and salt in a small bowl.

If using beefsteak tomatoes, cut the stems out to make a ½-inch cavity,
then cut a thin slice from each bottom so the tomatoes will stand level on the
grill. Fill each cavity with one-fourth of the garlic mixture. If using plum tomatoes,
halve lengthwise, then spoon the garlic mixture evenly onto the cut sides. Let
stand at room temperature for 1 hour.

Spray the grill rack with nonstick spray; prepare the grill for a medium fire using
the direct method (see page 81).

Place the beefsteak tomatoes along the edges of the grill rack and grill until hot,
15–20 minutes. If using plum tomatoes, thread the tomatoes onto 4 (12-inch)
metal skewers and place the skewers along the edges of the grill rack; grill until
hot, about 5 minutes. Serve the tomatoes hot or at room temperature.

PER SERVING (1 beefsteak tomato or 4 plum tomato halves): 57 Cal, 4 g Fat, 1 g Sat Fat,
0 g Trans Fat, 0 mg Chol, 43 mg Sod, 6 g Carb, 1 g Fib, 1 g Prot, 14 mg Calc. **POINTS** value: *1.*

Cucumber Wedges with Dill Dressing

If you've never tasted cooked cucumber, you're in for a pleasant surprise—it tastes completely different, yet delicious, when cooked. Served warm, it's an excellent side dish with salmon or lamb; chilled, it goes well with cold meat, fish, or poultry. If you serve this cold, sprinkle it with an additional teaspoon of minced fresh dill.

MAKES 4 SERVINGS

- ½ cup very thinly sliced onion
- 3 tablespoons white-wine vinegar
- 2 teaspoons minced fresh dill
- 1 large garlic clove, peeled and bruised
- ½ teaspoon sugar
- ¼ teaspoon salt
- ¼ teaspoon freshly ground pepper
- 2 cucumbers, peeled, seeded, and quartered lengthwise

To make the dressing, combine the onion, vinegar, dill, garlic, sugar, salt, and pepper in a large bowl. Let stand for at least 1 hour to blend the flavors. Remove and discard the garlic.

Spray the grill rack with nonstick spray; prepare the grill for a medium fire using the direct method (see page 81).

Place the cucumber wedges along the edges of the grill rack and grill, turning often, just until heated through, about 4 minutes. Transfer the hot cucumber wedges to the bowl with the dressing; toss well. Serve warm or cover and refrigerate 1–2 hours and serve chilled.

PER SERVING (2 cucumber wedges and 1 tablespoon dressing): 20 Cal, 0 g Fat, 0 g Sat Fat, 0 g Trans Fat, 0 mg Chol, 139 mg Sod, 5 g Carb, 1 g Fib, 1 g Prot, 15 mg Calc. *POINTS* value: *0.*

✓ Baby Artichokes with Garlic and Lemon

Baby artichokes—about the size of large walnuts—are incredibly delicious when grilled to a crispy brown. Eat them whole, leaves and all!

MAKES 4 SERVINGS 🌱

1–1¼ pounds baby artichokes
½ lemon
6–8 cups ice water
¼ cup fresh lemon juice

2 garlic cloves, minced
¼ teaspoon salt
¼ teaspoon freshly
**   ground pepper**

Prepare the grill for a medium fire using the direct method (see page 81). Spray a grill basket with nonstick spray.

Trim ⅛ inch off the tops and bottoms of the artichokes and remove any loose or discolored leaves. Slice the artichokes in half lengthwise through the heart. Rub each half with the cut side of the lemon.

Bring a large saucepan of water to a boil; drop in the artichokes and cook for 1 minute. With a slotted spoon, transfer the artichokes to a large bowl of ice water to stop the cooking; drain when completely cooled.

Combine the cooked artichokes, lemon juice, garlic, salt, and pepper in a medium bowl; toss well.

Place as many artichokes as will fit in a single layer in the grill basket. Place the grill basket on the grill rack and grill until crisp, brown, and tender, about 9 minutes on each side. Transfer the artichokes to a platter; cover with foil to keep warm. Repeat with the remaining artichokes.

PER SERVING (about 1 cup): 38 Cal, 0 g Fat, 0 g Sat Fat, 0 g Trans Fat, 0 mg Chol, 179 mg Sod, 8 g Carb, 3 g Fib, 2 g Prot, 22 mg Calc. *POINTS* value: *0.*

Charred Eggplant and Tomato with Goat Cheese

Eggplant, with its meaty texture, is perfect for grilling—and it combines beautifully with tomatoes. This Italian-style dish makes a great side dish with steaks or burgers and can even be served as a light main course accompanied by orzo or rice.

MAKES 4 SERVINGS

- ½ yellow bell pepper, seeded and diced
- ¼ cup reduced-sodium chicken broth
- 1 tablespoon + 1 teaspoon olive oil
- 1 tablespoon balsamic vinegar
- 2 garlic cloves, minced
- ¼ teaspoon salt
- ¼ teaspoon freshly ground pepper
- 1 eggplant, peeled and cut into 1-inch-thick slices
- 1 tomato, cut into ½-inch-thick slices
- ¾ cup crumbled goat cheese
- ¼ cup coarsely chopped basil

Place the bell pepper, broth, oil, vinegar, garlic, salt, and pepper in a food processor or blender and puree until smooth. Place the eggplant and tomato slices on a plate and brush both sides of each slice, with the bell pepper mixture. Let stand at room temperature, about 20 minutes.

Meanwhile, spray the grill rack with nonstick spray; prepare the grill for a medium fire using the direct method (see page 81).

Place the eggplant slices on the grill rack and grill until lightly charred, about 4 minutes on each side. Place the tomatoes on the grill rack and grill until lightly charred, about 2 minutes on each side.

Transfer the grilled eggplant and tomato to a serving platter, arranging the slices alternately and overlapping them. Sprinkle the cheese and basil evenly over the grilled vegetables.

PER SERVING (about 2 slices eggplant, 1 slice tomato, and 3 tablespoons cheese): 161 Cal, 11 g Fat, 5 g Sat Fat, 0 g Trans Fat, 17 mg Chol, 260 mg Sod, 11 g Carb, 2 g Fib, 7 g Prot, 124 mg Calc. *POINTS* value: *4.*

Herbed Portobello Mushroom Caps

Fresh herbs make all the difference to the flavor of this dish. If you don't have fresh basil, try fresh oregano or tarragon before resorting to the dried. This makes a delectable side dish with grilled chicken or steak. It's also a terrific appetizer.

MAKES 4 SERVINGS

¼ cup Madeira wine

1 tablespoon balsamic vinegar

1 tablespoon extra-virgin olive oil

1 tablespoon light tamari or reduced-sodium soy sauce

1 garlic clove, minced

2 tablespoons minced fresh basil, or 2 teaspoons dried

1 tablespoon minced fresh parsley

4 Portobello mushroom caps

Combine the wine, vinegar, oil, tamari, garlic, basil, and parsley in a zip-close plastic bag; add the mushrooms. Squeeze out the air and seal the bag; turn to coat the mushrooms. Refrigerate, turning the bag occasionally, at least 6 hours or overnight.

Spray the grill rack with nonstick spray; prepare the grill for a medium fire using the direct method (see page 81).

Transfer the mushrooms from the marinade to a plate. Reserve any remaining marinade. Place the mushrooms, stem-side down, on the grill rack and grill, turning occasionally, until golden brown, about 7 minutes. Transfer the mushrooms to a serving platter and drizzle with the marinade.

PER SERVING (1 mushroom cap): 69 Cal, 4 g Fat, 1 g Sat Fat, 0 g Trans Fat, 0 mg Chol, 154 mg Sod, 5 g Carb, 1 g Fib, 2 g Prot, 11 mg Calc. *POINTS* value: *2.*

TIP Tamari, similar to soy sauce, has a mild and distinctive flavor. It is available in Asian food markets, specialty food shops, and some supermarkets. Portobello mushroom stems can be woody, so remove them before grilling the caps. You can use the stems to flavor sauces or soups, if you like.

☑ Nutmeg Carrots

Garlic, a hint of nutmeg, and a glowing grill give these carrots rich flavor. Serve them hot with grilled chicken or turkey, or let them cool and toss them in a salad.

MAKES 4 SERVINGS 🥕

6 carrots, diagonally sliced ¼-inch thick (about 4 cups)

3 garlic cloves, peeled and halved

1 tablespoon water

2 teaspoons olive oil

¼ teaspoon salt

¼ teaspoon freshly ground pepper

⅛ teaspoon ground nutmeg

Prepare the grill for a medium fire using the direct method (see page 81).

Combine the carrots, garlic, water, oil, salt, pepper, and nutmeg in a small bowl. Transfer the carrot mixture to the center of a double layer of heavy-duty, extra-wide foil, about 24-inches long. Make a packet by bringing 2 sides of the foil up to meet in the center, and pressing the edges together to two ½-inch folds. Then fold the edges of each end together to two ½-inch folds. Allowing room for the packet to expand, crimp the edges together to seal.

Place the packet on the grill rack and grill until cooked through, about 25 minutes. Remove the packet from the grill and open it carefully to allow the hot steam to escape. Place in a serving dish or divide equally among 4 plates.

PER SERVING (¾ cup): 76 Cal, 2 g Fat, 0 g Sat Fat, 0 g Trans Fat, 0 mg Chol, 175 mg Sod, 13 g Carb, 4 g Fib, 2 g Prot, 42 mg Calc. **POINTS** value: *1.*

☑ Minted Green Beans

This recipe is easily doubled or tripled. Serve some hot off the grill and refrigerate some for up to 5 days. They make a great cold salad or part of a packed lunch.

MAKES 4 SERVINGS ⏱ 🥕

½ **pound fresh green beans,**
  trimmed
1 **tablespoon minced fresh mint**
1 **tablespoon fresh lemon juice**

2 **teaspoons olive oil**
¼ **teaspoon salt**
⅛ **teaspoon freshly**
  ground pepper

Prepare the grill for a medium fire using the direct method (see page 81).

Combine the beans, mint, lemon juice, oil, salt, and pepper in a medium bowl. Transfer the bean mixture to the center of a double layer of heavy-duty, extra-wide foil, about 24-inches long. Make a packet by bringing 2 sides of the foil up to meet in the center, and pressing the edges together to two ½-inch folds. Then fold the edges of each end together to two ½-inch folds. Allowing room for the packet to expand, crimp the edges together to seal.

Place the packet on the grill rack and grill until cooked through, about 15 minutes. Remove the packet from the grill and open it carefully to allow the hot steam to escape. Place in a serving dish or divide equally among 4 plates.

PER SERVING (½ cup) 38 Cal, 2 g Fat, 0 g Sat Fat, 0 g Trans Fat, 0 mg Chol, 139 mg Sod, 4 g Carb, 0 g Fib, 1 g Prot, 22 mg Calc. **POINTS** value: *1.*

Kale with Garlic and Balsamic

Kale cooked on the grill? Yes, this inventive way of cooking greens gives them flavor while steaming them ever so gently. Other possible choices are radicchio, beet greens, mustard greens, broccoli rabe, Swiss chard, sorrel, dandelion greens, spinach, or watercress.

MAKES 4 SERVINGS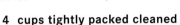

4   cups tightly packed cleaned and trimmed kale

2   tablespoons water

1   tablespoon olive oil

1   tablespoon balsamic vinegar

3   garlic cloves, minced

¼   teaspoon salt

¼   teaspoon freshly ground pepper

Prepare the grill for a medium fire using the direct method (see page 81).

Combine the kale, water, oil, vinegar, garlic, salt, and pepper in a medium bowl. Transfer the kale mixture to the center of a double layer of heavy-duty, extra-wide foil, about 24-inches long. Make a packet by bringing 2 sides of the foil up to meet in the center, and pressing the edges together to two ½-inch folds. Then fold the edges of each end together to two ½-inch folds. Allowing room for the packet to expand, crimp the edges together to seal.

Place the packet on the grill rack and grill until cooked through, 10–12 minutes. Remove the packet from the grill and open it carefully to allow the hot steam to escape. Place in a serving dish or divide equally among 4 plates.

PER SERVING (½ cup): 100 Cal, 4 g Fat, 1 g Sat Fat, 0 g Trans Fat, 0 mg Chol, 194 mg Sod, 14 g Carb, 9 g Fib, 5 g Prot, 187 mg Calc. **POINTS** value: **2.**

Fennel-Stuffed Onions

Use the sweetest onions you can find—such as Vidalia, Maui, or Walla Walla—for this delicious side dish. This is perfect for heartier grilled meats such as beef or pork.

MAKES 4 SERVINGS

- 4 large onions
- 2 teaspoons canola oil
- 1½ cups diced fennel
- ¼ teaspoon salt
- ⅛ teaspoon freshly ground pepper
- ½ cup chopped kale
- 4 teaspoons plain dry bread crumbs

Spray the grill rack with nonstick spray; prepare the grill for a medium fire using the direct method (see page 81).

Slice ½ inch off the top of each onion; scoop out the center, leaving 3 outer layers of the shell. Be careful not to cut through the bottom root. Dice the tops and centers of the onions and set aside.

Heat the oil in a medium saucepan over medium-high heat. Add the diced onions, fennel, salt, and pepper; cook, stirring frequently, until softened, about 12 minutes. Add the kale and cook until the vegetables are wilted and soft, about 4 minutes. Remove the pan from the heat and set aside.

Spray the onion shells lightly with nonstick spray. Place the onion shells on the grill rack, hollow-side down. Grill, turning frequently with tongs, until they begin to soften, 7–10 minutes.

Transfer the onion shells to a platter. Spoon one-fourth of the vegetable mixture into the cavity of each onion. Top each with 1 teaspoon of the bread crumbs. Place the stuffed onions back on the edges of the grill rack and grill, keeping the heat medium-low, until the stuffed onions are golden brown, about 30 minutes.

PER SERVING (1 stuffed onion): 68 Cal, 2 g Fat, 0 g Sat Fat, 0 g Trans Fat, 0 mg Chol, 217 mg Sod, 11 g Carb, 3 g Fib, 2 g Prot, 53 mg Calc. ***POINTS*** value: *1.*

☑ Whole Beets with Thyme

Roasting beets this way brings out their natural sweetness while giving them a subtle herb flavor. They go beautifully with chicken, turkey, or game.

MAKES 4 SERVINGS 🌱

2 teaspoons minced fresh thyme

2 teaspoons olive oil

¼ teaspoon salt

¼ teaspoon freshly ground pepper

4 peeled trimmed beets
   (about ¾ pound)

Prepare the grill for a medium fire using the direct method (see page 81).

Combine the thyme, oil, salt, and pepper in a small bowl. Transfer 1 beet to the center of a double layer of heavy-duty, extra-wide foil, about 6-inches long. Drizzle one-fourth of the thyme mixture over the beet. Make a packet by bringing 2 sides of the foil up to meet in the center, and pressing the edges together to two ½-inch folds. Then fold the edges of each end together to two ½-inch folds. Allowing room for the packet to expand, crimp the edges together to seal. Repeat with the remaining beets.

Place the packets on the grill rack and grill until cooked through, about 40 minutes. Remove the packets from the grill and open carefully to allow the hot steam to escape. Place the beets in a serving dish or place one on each of 4 plates.

PER SERVING (1 beet): 47 Cal, 2 g Fat, 0 g Sat Fat, 0 g Trans Fat, 0 mg Chol, 178 mg Sod, 6 g Carb, 1 g Fib, 1 g Prot, 14 mg Calc. *POINTS* value: *1.*

Apple and Raisin–Stuffed Squash

Golden onions, apple, celery, and raisins make a delicious old-fashioned stuffing for this favorite autumn vegetable, made more delicious by cooking it on the grill.

MAKES 4 SERVINGS

2 teaspoons canola oil
1 onion, chopped
1 apple, cored and diced
¾ cup diced celery

¼ cup golden raisins
2 (1-pound) acorn squashes, rinsed, halved, and seeded

Spray the grill rack with nonstick spray; prepare the grill for a low fire using the direct method (see page 81).

To make the stuffing, heat the oil in a medium saucepan over medium-high heat. Add the onion and cook, stirring constantly, until golden, about 5 minutes. Add the apple, celery, and raisins; cook, stirring frequently, until softened, about 6 minutes. Remove the pan from the heat and set aside.

Place the squash halves on the grill rack cut-side down and grill for 10 minutes.

Transfer the squash halves to a plate and fill the cavities evenly with the filling. Return the squash, cut-side up, to the grill rack. Cover the grill and cook until the stuffed squash halves are soft and lightly browned, about 40 minutes.

PER SERVING (½ stuffed squash): 179 Cal, 3 g Fat, 0 g Sat Fat, 0 mg Chol, 29 mg Sod, 40 g Carb, 9 g Fib, 3 g Prot, 92 mg Calc. **POINTS** value: **3.**

Mediterranean-Style Stuffed Zucchini

Zucchini is hollowed out, stuffed with a delicious rice, onion, tomato and cheese mixture, then sliced into pretty, bite-size rounds.

MAKES 4 SERVINGS

- 2 zucchini (about ½ pound each)
- 1 teaspoon extra-virgin olive oil
- ½ cup chopped onion
- ½ cup chopped plum tomatoes
- 2 garlic cloves, minced
- ½ cup cooked white rice, cooled
- 6 large kalamata olives, pitted and chopped
- ⅛ teaspoon freshly ground pepper
- 3 tablespoons chopped fresh basil
- 2 teaspoons grated Parmesan cheese

Spray the grill rack with nonstick spray; prepare the grill for a medium fire using the direct method (see page 81).

Trim the ends from each zucchini; cut each zucchini in half crosswise. With a sharp paring knife, cut a hole lengthwise through each zucchini half; insert the knife tip and turn it until the inner flesh loosens. Remove the inner flesh, hollowing out the zucchini from end to end to form a tube. Chop the inner flesh that has been removed; set aside.

To make the stuffing, heat the oil in a medium nonstick skillet over medium heat. Add the onion and cook, stirring constantly, until translucent, about 5 minutes. Add the reserved chopped zucchini, the tomatoes, and garlic; cook, stirring constantly, about 1 minute. Stir in the rice, olives, and pepper; cook, stirring constantly, until heated through, about 1 minute. Remove the stuffing from the heat; stir in the basil and cheese. Let the mixture cool slightly. Using your fingers, stuff one-fourth of the mixture tightly into each zucchini cavity.

Place the stuffed zucchini halves on the grill rack and grill, turning occasionally, until well browned and heated through, about 20 minutes. Transfer the zucchini to a cutting board and cut each piece into 6 (about ½-inch) round slices.

PER SERVING (6 slices stuffed zucchini): 102 Cal, 4 g Fat, 1 g Sat Fat, 0 g Trans Fat, 1 mg Chol, 255 mg Sod, 15 g Carb, 1 g Fib, 3 g Prot, 61 mg Calc. *POINTS* value: *2.*

MEDITERRANEAN-STYLE STUFFED ZUCCHINI

SUMMER VEGETABLES
WITH ROASTED GARLIC

Summer Vegetables with Roasted Garlic

This mélange of zucchini, tomatoes, eggplant, and bell peppers receives an irresistibly earthy, smoky flavor from the grill. Make it a day ahead if you like and serve it cold, hot, or at room temperature. Leftovers make a wonderful pasta sauce or a superb filling for an omelette or sandwich. Make it often to keep some on hand all summer long.

MAKES 8 SERVINGS

2 tablespoons + 2 teaspoons extra-virgin olive oil

2–4 tablespoons slivered fresh basil

1 tablespoon red-wine vinegar

½ teaspoon salt

½ teaspoon freshly ground pepper

2 large onions, peeled (do not cut root end) and quartered

4 small zucchini, scrubbed and cut into 1-inch chunks

12 large plum tomatoes, halved lengthwise

1 eggplant, peeled and cut into 1-inch cubes

1 red bell pepper, seeded and cut into eighths

1 green bell pepper, seeded and cut into eighths

1 head Grill-Roasted Garlic (page 209)

Spray the grill rack with nonstick spray; prepare the grill for a medium fire using the direct method (see page 81). If you are using wooden skewers, soak them in water for 30 minutes.

To make the vinaigrette, combine the oil, basil, vinegar, salt, and ground pepper in a large bowl; set aside.

Thread the onions, zucchini, tomatoes, eggplant, and bell peppers separately onto 12 (12-inch) metal or wooden skewers (approximately 2 skewers per vegetable). Place the skewers on the grill rack and grill, turning frequently, until very lightly charred, about 6 minutes for the zucchini and eggplant, about 9 minutes for the tomatoes and bell peppers, and about 12 minutes for the onions. As the vegetables are done, slide them off their skewers and into the bowl with the vinaigrette, tossing the vegetables lightly after each addition.

Cut the top from the roasted garlic head and squeeze the pulp directly onto the grilled vegetables. Toss again to coat.

PER SERVING (1 cup): 110 Cal, 5 g Fat, 1 g Sat Fat, 0 g Trans Fat, 0 mg Chol, 151 mg Sod, 16 g Carb, 3 g Fib, 3 g Prot, 64 mg Calc. *POINTS* value: *2.*

SAFETY FIRST

• Never use a charcoal or gas grill indoors. Keep all grills away from anything flammable, including dry grass, hanging tree limbs, and the garage.

• Clean out the ash pan of a charcoal grill only when the grill is completely cool—a hot ember could start a fire in the garbage can. Scrub the grill grid with a wire brush to get rid of food particles.

• Open the gas grill lid before lighting.

• Spray the grill rack with nonstick spray before lighting the grill. Do not spray the grill rack while the grill is alight; a dangerous flare-up could result.

• Do not use kerosene or gasoline to light coals; use only starter fluid—and never add starter fluid to quick-lighting briquettes or hot coals.

• Never wear clothing with puffy sleeves, flowing skirts, long scarves, or any other pieces that might easily catch fire.

• Keep a spray bottle full of water handy to extinguish minor flare-ups.

• Never leave a hot grill unattended, especially around children and pets.

• Don't leave the coals burning when you have finished grilling; douse them in water and stir until the fire is completely out.

• Store propane cylinders and starter fluids outdoors, upright, and away from children. Keep out of sunlight or enclosed areas.

• Trim as much fat as possible from meats and poultry before grilling; fat dripping on the grill can cause flare-ups. If a fire occurs, cover the grill tightly until the flames subside.

• Transfer cooked food from the grill to a clean plate to prevent cross contamination with the plate that brought the raw food to the grill.

• Always marinate meat, poultry, and fish in the refrigerator. Do not let them stand more than 30 minutes at room temperature before grilling.

• If you are using any leftover marinade from meat, poultry, or fish to serve with or brush on the grilled food, be sure to boil the marinade for 3 minutes to prevent bacteria growth. If you are not using it immediately, remove it from the heat, let it cool to room temperature, and refrigerate it.

✓ Layered Eggplant and Bell Peppers

These colorful roasted bell peppers, eggplant, and scallions, drizzled with a fresh herbed dressing look especially appealing if you layer them in a shallow glass dish.

MAKES 4 SERVINGS 🌶

2 assorted color bell peppers, seeded and quartered

1 eggplant, peeled and thinly sliced

8 scallions, trimmed

2 tablespoons red-wine vinegar

1 tablespoon olive oil

1 tablespoon water

1 tablespoon chopped fresh oregano

1 tablespoon chopped fresh basil

Pinch salt

Freshly ground pepper, to taste

Spray the grill rack with nonstick spray; prepare the grill for a medium fire using the direct method (see page 81).

Place the bell peppers on the grill rack and grill until slightly charred and tender, about 5 minutes on each side. Place the eggplant on the grill rack and grill until slightly charred and tender, 2-3 minutes on each side. Place the scallions on the grill rack and grill until slightly charred and tender, 1-2 minutes on each side.

To make the vinaigrette, whisk together the vinegar, oil, water, oregano, basil, salt, and ground pepper in a small bowl. Set aside.

Transfer the grilled vegetables to a cutting board; slice the scallions into 2-inch pieces. In a wide, shallow serving dish, alternate layers of the eggplant, bell peppers, and scallions, drizzling a small amount of the vinaigrette over each layer, and drizzling the remaining vinaigrette over the top. Cover the dish with plastic wrap, and refrigerate at least 1 hour to allow the flavors to blend. Serve slightly chilled or at room temperature.

PER SERVING (½ cup mixed vegetables and about 1 tablespoon dressing): 81 Cal, 4 g Fat, 0 g Sat Fat, 0 g Trans Fat, 0 mg Chol, 41 mg Sod, 12 g Carb, 3 g Fib, 2 g Prot, 62 mg Calc.
POINTS value: *1.*

☑ Spicy Potato Wedges

Sprinkled with malt or cider vinegar, or topped with a dollop of fat-free sour cream, these crispy potatoes are also delicious unembellished.

MAKES 4 SERVINGS

- 1 tablespoon + 1 teaspoon olive oil
- ½ teaspoon salt
- ¼ teaspoon cayenne, or to taste
- ¼ teaspoon garlic powder
- 4 (5-ounce) baking potatoes, scrubbed and quartered lengthwise

Spray the grill rack with nonstick spray; prepare the grill for a medium fire using the direct method (see page 81).

Combine the oil, salt, cayenne, and garlic powder in a medium bowl; add the potatoes and toss to coat.

Place the potato wedges along the edges of the grill rack. Grill, turning every 7 minutes, moving the wedges closer to the center of the grill rack with each turn, until the potatoes are tender and lightly browned, about 20 minutes. Serve at once.

PER SERVING (4 potato wedges): 147 Cal, 5 g Fat, 1 g Sat Fat, 0 g Trans Fat, 0 mg Chol, 302 mg Sod, 25 g Carb, 3 g Fib, 3 g Prot, 18 mg Calc. *POINTS* value: *3.*

TIP Use long-handled tongs to turn the potatoes and a long-handled barbecue fork to test when the potatoes are tender.

Grill-Roasted Garlic Mashed Potatoes

Mashed potatoes get a fat-free, buttery-sweet flavor from grill-roasted garlic. The roasting has a taming effect on the garlic and turns an otherwise ordinary side dish into a delicious, healthful treat.

MAKES 8 SERVINGS

2½ pounds baking potatoes, peeled and cut into 1-inch cubes

2 heads Grill-Roasted Garlic (see page 209)

½ cup hot fat-free milk

½ cup hot evaporated fat-free milk

½ teaspoon salt

¼ teaspoon freshly ground pepper

Place the potatoes and cold water to cover in a large saucepan; bring to a boil. Reduce the heat and simmer, uncovered, just until tender, 10–15 minutes. Drain, reserving the liquid. Return the potatoes to the saucepan and shake over low heat until the potatoes appear floury, about 2 minutes.

Slice the tops off the roasted garlic heads and squeeze the pulp out of each clove into a large bowl.

Force the potatoes and roasted garlic through a ricer or food mill into a medium bowl. Whisk in the milk, evaporated milk, salt, and pepper. Thin to desired consistency with 1 or 2 tablespoons of the reserved potato water. Serve at once.

PER SERVING (1 cup): 127 Cal, 0 g Fat, 0 g Sat Fat, 0 g Trans Fat, 1 mg Chol, 174 mg Sod, 27 g Carb, 2 g Fib, 5 g Prot, 93 mg Calc. **POINTS** value: *2.*

TIP If you don't have a ricer or food mill, simply mash the potatoes with the garlic, milks, and seasonings in the saucepan, using a hand-held electric mixer or a potato masher.

Grilled Sweet Potatoes with Lime

These sweet potatoes are not only simple to make they are also utterly delicious. Use the lighter-skinned variety of sweet potato rather than the orange-red type (often labeled yams). This is the perfect accompaniment to Chicken with Lemon, Ginger, and Basil (page 67).

MAKES 4 SERVINGS

4 (6-ounce) sweet potatoes, well scrubbed

4 lime wedges
Minced fresh cilantro, to taste

Prepare the grill for a medium fire using the direct method.

When the coals are covered with white ash, bury the potatoes in the coals and roast, turning once, until the potatoes can be pierced easily with a barbecue fork, about 45 minutes.

Transfer the potatoes to each of 4 plates. Cut the potatoes in half and scoop out the pulp, discarding the charred skins. Serve with a squeeze of lime juice and sprinkle lightly with the cilantro.

PER SERVING (½ cup): 129 Cal, 0 g Fat, 0 g Sat Fat, 0 g Trans Fat, 0 mg Chol, 16 mg Sod, 30 g Carb, 4 g Fib, 2 g Prot, 27 mg Calc. **POINTS** value: **2.**

Sweet-and-Spicy Sweet Potatoes

Serve these barbecue-flavored treats as a side dish with burgers or grilled chicken, or even as an appetizer after a day of hiking or skiing.

MAKES 4 SERVINGS

- 2 tablespoons + 2 teaspoons ketchup
- 1 tablespoon Worcestershire sauce
- 1 tablespoon red-wine vinegar

- 1 teaspoon yellow mustard
- ½ teaspoon freshly ground pepper
- 1 pound sweet potatoes, peeled and cut lengthwise into ¼-inch-thick slices

Spray the grill rack with nonstick spray; prepare the grill for a medium fire using the direct method (see page 81).

Combine the ketchup, Worcestershire sauce, vinegar, mustard, and pepper in a small bowl; mix well.

Brush the potato slices on both sides with the ketchup mixture. Place the potato slices on the grill rack and grill, turning frequently with tongs and brushing with the remaining ketchup mixture, about 8 minutes. Serve hot.

PER SERVING (about 4 slices): 104 Cal, 0 g Fat, 0 g Sat Fat, 0 g Trans Fat, 0 mg Chol, 188 mg Sod, 24 g Carb, 3 g Fib, 2 g Prot, 25 mg Calc. **POINTS** value: **1.**

Salad Entrées and Salad Sides

Grilled Shrimp, Snow Pea, and Rice Salad

This elegant salad is a marvelous blend of sweet-and-sour Asian flavors.

MAKES 4 SERVINGS

⅓ cup + 2 tablespoons pineapple juice

2 tablespoons reduced-sodium soy sauce

2 tablespoons dry sherry

1 garlic clove, minced

½ teaspoon ground ginger

16 medium shrimp (about ½ pound), peeled and deveined

2 teaspoons Asian (dark) sesame oil

½ teaspoon fresh lemon juice

2 cups cooked white rice, cooled

1 cup snow peas, cut into ½-inch lengths

½ cup fresh pineapple, peeled and diced

¼ cup sliced scallions

Spray the grill rack with nonstick spray; prepare the grill for a medium fire using the direct method (see page 81). If using wooden skewers, soak them in water for 30 minutes.

Combine ⅓ cup of the pineapple juice, the soy sauce, sherry, half of the garlic, and ¼ teaspoon of the ginger in a zip-close plastic bag; reserve 2 tablespoons of the mixture in a medium bowl for the dressing. Add the shrimp to the plastic bag; squeeze out the air and seal the bag. Turn to coat the shrimp. Refrigerate for 20 minutes. Remove the shrimp; discard the marinade.

Thread 4 shrimp onto each of 4 (12-inch) metal or wooden skewers. Place the skewers on the grill rack and grill, turning occasionally, until opaque in the center, about 4 minutes. Let cool. Remove the shrimp from the skewers, halve each shrimp lengthwise, and set aside.

To make the dressing, whisk the remaining 2 tablespoons pineapple juice, the oil, lemon juice, the remaining garlic, and ¼ teaspoon ginger into the reserved 2 tablespoons marinade.

Combine the rice, snow peas, pineapple, scallions, and reserved shrimp in a separate medium bowl; drizzle the dressing over the salad and toss to coat. Cover and refrigerate at least 1 hour to allow the flavors to blend.

PER SERVING (about 1¼ cups): 266 Cal, 4 g Fat, 1 g Sat Fat, 0 g Trans Fat, 86 mg Chol, 389 mg Sod, 39 g Carb, 1 g Fib, 16 g Prot, 64 mg Calc. *POINTS* value: *5.*

GRILLED SHRIMP, SNOW PEA, AND RICE SALAD

☑ Tuna Niçoise Salad

Salade Niçoise—a classic dish from the Provençal region in southern France—is made extra delicious by grilling the tuna.

MAKES 6 SERVINGS

2 tablespoons fresh lemon juice
1 tablespoon white-wine vinegar
2 teaspoons Dijon mustard
1 tablespoon olive oil
2 (10-ounce) tuna steaks
½ teaspoon salt
¼ teaspoon freshly ground pepper
1¼ pounds small new potatoes, scrubbed and halved

1 cup fresh green beans, trimmed
6 cups torn romaine lettuce leaves
2 tomatoes, each cut into sixths
10 small pitted black olives, halved
¼ cup minced fresh basil

Spray the grill rack with nonstick spray; prepare the grill for a medium-hot fire using the direct method (see page 81).

To make the dressing, combine the lemon juice, vinegar, and mustard in a small bowl; whisk in the oil a little at a time. Set aside.

Sprinkle the tuna steaks with the salt and pepper and place on the grill rack. Grill until cooked through, about 4 minutes on each side. Cool the tuna to room temperature, then cut into ¼-inch-thick slices or break into chunks.

Place the potatoes in a medium saucepan, cover with cold water and simmer until tender, about 20 minutes. Drain and let cool.

Bring 2 inches of water to a boil in a medium saucepan. Arrange the beans on a steamer rack; place the steamer rack in the saucepan and steam until crisp-tender, about 5 minutes. Rinse under cold water until completely cooled.

Arrange the lettuce on a large serving platter. Place the potatoes around the edge of the lettuce; arrange the beans along the inside edge of the potatoes. Place the tomatoes along the inside edge of the beans, and mound the tuna in the center. Spread the olives around the rim. Sprinkle the basil over the salad and drizzle with the dressing.

PER SERVING (⅙ of salad): 233 Cal, 5 g Fat, 1 g Sat Fat, 0 g Trans Fat, 44 mg Chol, 383 mg Sod, 19 g Carb, 4 g Fib, 27 g Prot, 63 mg Calc. **POINTS** value: **4.**

Grilled Steak and Potato Salad

MAKES 4 SERVINGS

- 1 **cup tomato juice**
- 2 **tablespoons red-wine vinegar**
- 1 **tablespoon chili powder**
- 1 **tablespoon Worcestershire sauce**
- ¼ **teaspoon sugar**
- ¼ **teaspoon cayenne or hot pepper sauce**

- 1 **(¾-pound) lean flank steak, pierced on both sides with a fork**
- 8 **(2-ounce) new potatoes, scrubbed**
- 2 **small–medium yellow onions, peeled and left whole**
- 12 **cherry tomatoes, halved**

Spray the grill rack with nonstick spray; prepare the grill for a medium fire using the direct method (see page 81).

Combine ¾ cup of the tomato juice, the vinegar, chili powder, Worcestershire sauce, sugar, and cayenne in a zip-close plastic bag; reserve 3 tablespoons of the mixture in a small bowl for the dressing. Add the steak to the plastic bag; squeeze out the air and seal the bag. Turn to coat the steak. Refrigerate, turning the bag once, about 1 hour.

Place the potatoes, onions, and cold water to cover in a saucepan. Simmer until barely tender, about 8 minutes. Drain and let cool. Halve the potatoes and onions. Thread 4 potato halves and 1 onion half onto each of 4 (12-inch) metal skewers.

Remove the steak from the marinade. Discard the marinade. Place the steak on the grill rack and grill, turning once, until an instant-read thermometer inserted in the center of the steak registers 145°F for medium-rare, 4–5 minutes on each side, or 160°F for medium, 5–6 minutes on each side. Place the vegetables on the grill rack and grill, turning occasionally, until tender and lightly browned, about 8 minutes. Transfer the steak and vegetables to a cutting board; let the steak stand 5 minutes, then cut across the grain into thin diagonal slices. Chop the cooked potatoes and onions into chunks. Place the steak, potatoes, and onions in a serving bowl; add the tomatoes.

Whisk the remaining ¼ cup tomato juice into the reserved 3 tablespoons marinade. Drizzle the dressing over the salad and toss gently to coat. Serve warm.

PER SERVING (about 1⅔ cups): 245 Cal, 7 g Fat, 3 g Sat Fat, 1 g Trans Fat, 41 mg Chol, 337 mg Sod, 24 g Carb, 4 g Fib, 21 g Prot, 34 mg Calc. *POINTS* value: *5.*

RICE, CARROT, AND
ZUCCHINI SALAD

Rice, Carrot, and Zucchini Salad

This delicious salad can be made a day ahead and stored, covered, in the refrigerator. Slice the vegetables on the diagonal for a pretty effect. For a touch of sweetness, add a few dried cranberries, currants, or raisins to the salad and remember to deduct them from your **weekly POINTS Allowance.**

MAKES 4 SERVINGS

1 cup short-grain brown rice
2¼ cups water
1 carrot, cut into ¼-inch slices
4 scallions, white and light green parts only, cut into 1-inch lengths
½ zucchini, cut into ¼-inch slices
½ cup reduced-sodium chicken broth

2 tablespoons fresh lemon juice
1 tablespoon + 1 teaspoon olive oil
1 teaspoon minced fresh thyme
½ teaspoon salt
¼ teaspoon freshly ground pepper
2 tablespoons minced fresh parsley

Combine the rice and 2 cups of the water in a medium saucepan; bring to a boil. Reduce the heat and simmer, covered, until the rice is tender, about 40 minutes. Remove the saucepan from the heat; uncover and let the rice cool.

Prepare the grill for a medium fire using the direct method (see page 81). Spray a grill basket with nonstick spray.

Meanwhile, bring the remaining ¼ cup water to a boil in a small saucepan. Add the carrot, reduce the heat, and simmer about 3 minutes; drain.

Layer the carrot, scallions, and zucchini in the grill basket; place the grill basket on the grill rack and grill until the vegetables are slightly charred and tender, about 3 minutes on each side. Transfer the grilled vegetables to a plate.

Whisk together the broth, lemon juice, oil, thyme, salt, and pepper in a small bowl; stir into the rice. Spoon the mixture onto a serving platter and top with the grilled vegetables. Sprinkle the salad with the parsley before serving.

PER SERVING (1 cup): 236 Cal, 6 g Fat, 1 g Sat Fat, 0 g Trans Fat, 0 mg Chol, 387 mg Sod, 45 g Carb, 4 g Fib, 5 g Prot, 27 mg Calc. **POINTS** value: **4.**

Summer Vegetable Pasta Salad

Grilled vegetables provide unique flavors and the piquant yogurt-and-orange dressing adds the right finishing touch to this satisfying salad.

MAKES 8 SERVINGS

¾ pound ziti or penne pasta

1 zucchini, cut lengthwise into ½-inch slices

½ small eggplant, peeled and cut lengthwise into ½-inch slices

1 red bell pepper, seeded and quartered

2 carrots, cut lengthwise into ¼-inch slices

½ cup finely chopped onion

¼ cup orange juice

2 tablespoons olive oil

1 tablespoon plain fat-free yogurt

1 teaspoon Dijon mustard

¼ teaspoon salt

Freshly ground pepper, to taste

Prepare the grill for a hot fire using the direct method (see page 81). Spray a grill basket with nonstick spray.

Cook the pasta according to package directions, omitting the salt. Drain, rinse, and drain again. Place the pasta in a serving bowl; set aside and keep warm.

Place the zucchini, eggplant, bell pepper, and carrots in the grill basket; place the grill basket on the grill. Grill the vegetables until slightly charred and tender, 4–5 minutes on each side. Transfer the grilled vegetables to a cutting board, let cool slightly, then cut into bite-size pieces. Add the grilled vegetables and the onion to the pasta.

Whisk together the orange juice, oil, yogurt, mustard, salt, and ground pepper in a small bowl. Drizzle the dressing over the pasta mixture and toss well to coat. Serve the salad warm.

PER SERVING (1 cup): 219 Cal, 4 g Fat, 1 g Sat Fat, 0 g Trans Fat, 0 mg Chol, 98 mg Sod, 39 g Carb, 3 g Fib, 7 g Prot, 33 mg Calc. *POINTS* value: *4.*

TIP You can substitute any medium-size tubular pasta for the ziti or penne, including macaroni, rotelle, or radiatore. You might also experiment with spinach-or tomato-flavored pasta.

Warm Radicchio with Basil Dressing

Grilling mellows the slightly bitter flavor of radicchio while fresh basil dressing brightens it. This is an elegant and unusual side dish for a festive dinner al fresco, and it goes particularly well with grilled chicken or turkey.

MAKES 4 SERVINGS

2 heads radicchio, trimmed and quartered	2 teaspoons extra-virgin olive oil
⅓ cup minced fresh basil	¼ teaspoon salt
2 tablespoons water	¼ teaspoon freshly ground pepper
1 tablespoon + 1 teaspoon balsamic vinegar	

Spray the grill rack with nonstick spray; prepare the grill for a medium fire using the direct method (see page 81).

Place the radicchio quarters on the grill rack and grill, turning once with tongs, until just cooked through, about 4 minutes on each side.

Meanwhile, to make the dressing, combine the basil, water, vinegar, oil, salt, and pepper in a small bowl.

Transfer 2 quarters of the grilled radicchio to each of 4 plates and drizzle evenly with the dressing.

PER SERVING (2 radicchio quarters and 1 tablespoon dressing): 33 Cal, 3 g Fat, 0 g Sat Fat, 0 g Trans Fat, 0 mg Chol, 140 mg Sod, 3 g Carb, 0 g Fib, 1 g Prot, 66 mg Calc. **POINTS** value: *1.*

Foil-Grilled Cabbage Slaw

This recipe is an unusual twist on traditional coleslaw. The flavors are similar, but it is made without mayonnaise for a lighter consistency and a fresher taste—and, the vegetables are grilled. Serve it with grilled steak, hamburgers, or pork.

MAKES 4 SERVINGS

1½ cups shredded green cabbage

1 cup shredded carrots

½ cup seeded and thinly sliced red bell pepper

½ cup thinly sliced red onion

2 teaspoons olive oil

2 teaspoons white-wine vinegar

1 teaspoon sugar

¼ teaspoon celery seeds

¼ teaspoon salt

Prepare the grill for a medium fire using the direct method (see page 81).

Combine the cabbage, carrots, bell pepper, onion, oil, vinegar, sugar, celery seeds, and salt in a medium bowl. Place about 18 inches of a double layer of heavy-duty, extra-wide foil on a counter. Transfer the vegetable mixture to the center of the foil; make a packet by bringing 2 sides of the foil up to meet in the center and pressing the edges together in two ½-inch folds. Then fold the edges of each end together in two ½-inch folds. Allowing room for the packet to expand, crimp the edges together to seal.

Place the packet on the grill rack, and grill until cooked through, 15–18 minutes. Remove the packet from the grill, and open it carefully, allowing the hot steam to escape. Serve hot or at room temperature.

PER SERVING (½ cup): 54 Cal, 2 g Fat, 0 g Sat Fat, 0 g Trans Fat, 0 mg Chol, 152 mg Sod, 8 g Carb, 2 g Fib, 1 g Prot, 30 mg Calc. *POINTS* value: *1.*

☑ Orange and Celery Salad

MAKES 6 SERVINGS ⊗ ⏱ ☞

3 small oranges

¼ cup fresh lime juice

1 tablespoon canola oil

½ teaspoon ground coriander

Freshly ground pepper, to taste

6 medium celery stalks,
    thinly sliced

1½ cups thinly sliced radishes

Peel each orange, including the white pith, with a paring knife. Cut the peeled orange horizontally into 1-inch slices. Stack the slices and cut them into quarters.

To make the dressing, whisk together the lime juice, oil, coriander, and pepper in a small bowl.

Place the orange pieces, celery, and radishes in a serving bowl. Drizzle the dressing over the oranges and vegetables and toss gently to coat.

PER SERVING (1 cup): 61 Cal, 3 g Fat, 0 g Sat Fat, 0 g Trans Fat, 0 mg Chol, 33 mg Sod, 10 g Carb, 3 g Fib, 1 g Prot, 46 mg Calc. *POINTS* value: *1.*

TOOLS OF THE TRADE

Fire Igniters—an electric fire starter, or a gun-shaped gas lighter that allows you to spark the prepared charcoal.

Wire Brush—essential for cleaning the grill rack before you start cooking.

Charcoal Chimney Starter—a cylindrical metal container that allows you to get charcoal going quickly without using lighter fluid, making it an environmentally smart choice.

Grill Basket—a rectangular basket, with small perforations or tightly spaced grids that allows you to grill small items, such as shellfish and vegetables.

Long-Handled Tongs, Forks, and Spatulas—to prevent you from burning your hands and arms. Long-handled gloves and basting brushes are also helpful.

Instant-Read Meat Thermometer—the quickest, most accurate tool to judge when meat or poultry is cooked.

Corn and Jicama Salad

This salad packs well for a go-along to a tailgate picnic, yet it is elegant enough for a dinner party. Jicama, a large root vegetable with a sweet nutty taste, is available in Hispanic grocery stores and many large supermarkets. You can substitute celery for the jicama, if you prefer.

MAKES 4 SERVINGS

1 tablespoon minced fresh dill

1 tablespoon fresh lemon juice

1 tablespoon Dijon mustard

½ teaspoon salt

½ teaspoon freshly ground pepper

½ garlic clove, minced

¼ cup carrot juice

1 tablespoon + 1 teaspoon olive oil

4 ears Grilled Corn on the Cob, kernels removed to make 2 cups (page 116)

1 cup diced jicama

½ cup chopped Garlicky Grilled Bell Peppers (page 119)

¼ cup chopped scallions

¼ cup minced fresh parsley

Combine the dill, lemon juice, mustard, salt, ground pepper, and garlic in a food processor or blender and puree. Add the carrot juice and, while the machine is running, slowly add the oil; continue to puree until the mixture is thick and smooth. Set aside.

Combine the corn, jicama, bell peppers, scallions, and parsley in a medium bowl. Drizzle the dressing over the vegetables and toss gently to coat.

PER SERVING (1 cup): 159 Cal, 6 g Fat, 1 g Sat Fat, 0 g Trans Fat, 0 mg Chol, 436 mg Sod, 27 g Carb, 4 g Fib, 3 g Prot, 32 mg Calc. *POINTS* value: *3.*

TIP Carrot juice is available in health-food stores and many supermarkets.

✅ Charred Endive, Radicchio, and Asparagus

You might like to try this salad in a sandwich, particularly between two slices of whole-grain rustic bread, spread with a little hummus. Remember to deduct the bread and hummus from your **weekly *POINTS* Allowance**. The vegetables will keep, tightly wrapped, in the refrigerator for several days.

MAKES 4 SERVINGS 🥕

- 2 tablespoons fresh lemon juice
- 2 tablespoons balsamic vinegar
- 1 teaspoon Dijon mustard
- 1 garlic clove, minced
- 1/2 teaspoon salt
- 1/4 teaspoon freshly ground pepper
- 1 tablespoon + 1 teaspoon olive oil

- 2 leeks, trimmed, well-washed, and cut into 1/4-inch slices
- 2 heads Belgian endive, trimmed and cut into 1/4-inch slices
- 2 heads radicchio, trimmed and cut into 1/4-inch slices
- 24 asparagus spears, trimmed
- 2 zucchini, cut into 1/4-inch slices

Prepare the grill for a medium fire using the direct method (see page 81). Spray a grill basket with nonstick spray.

To make the dressing, combine the lemon juice, vinegar, mustard, garlic, salt, and pepper in a small bowl; whisk in the oil a little at a time until the dressing is smooth. Set aside.

Arrange the leeks in a single layer in the grill basket. Place the basket on the grill rack, cover the grill, and cook 5 minutes on each side. Remove the cover and grill 2 minutes longer on each side. Transfer the leeks to a serving bowl or platter.

Repeat the grilling procedure with the endive, radicchio, asparagus, and zucchini, grilling each vegetable separately, covered, 3 minutes on each side; then uncovered, 1 minute on each side.

Transfer all the grilled vegetables to the serving bowl or platter. Drizzle the dressing over the vegetables and toss gently to coat. Serve warm or chilled.

PER SERVING (1 cup): 104 Cal, 5 g Fat, 1 g Sat Fat, 0 g Trans Fat, 0 mg Chol, 307 mg Sod, 13 g Carb, 3 g Fib, 5 g Prot, 71 mg Calc. ***POINTS* value: *2.***

✓ Warm Grilled Potatoes and Sweet Onions

Grilled new potatoes and Spanish onions, combine with a lightly spiced yogurt dressing, to make this salad a delightful and unique variation on the old-fashioned potato salad we all know.

MAKES 4 SERVINGS

1¼ pounds new potatoes, cut into 1-inch slices	⅛ teaspoon cayenne
2 tablespoons white-wine vinegar	¾ cup yogurt cheese (see TIP below)
2 tablespoons fresh lemon juice	½ cup chopped scallions
1 garlic clove, minced	¼ cup minced fresh parsley
½ teaspoon salt	2 medium Spanish onions, separated into rings
¼ teaspoon paprika	

Spray the grill rack with nonstick spray; prepare the grill for a medium-hot fire using the direct method (see page 81). Spray a grill basket with nonstick spray.

Place the potatoes in cold water to cover in a medium saucepan and simmer until barely tender, about 15 minutes. Drain and set aside.

To make the dressing, combine the vinegar, lemon juice, garlic, salt, paprika, and cayenne in a food processor or blender; pulse several times to mix. Add the yogurt cheese and puree just until the dressing is smooth. Transfer to a medium bowl; stir in the scallions and parsley and set aside.

Place the potatoes and the onion rings in the grill basket. Place the grill basket on the grill rack and grill, turning frequently, until the onions are tender and the potatoes are browned, about 9 minutes.

Transfer the grilled vegetables to a cutting board. Add the potatoes to the dressing in the bowl. Coarsely chop the grilled onions, add them to the bowl, and toss well. Serve the salad warm.

PER SERVING (1 cup): 170 Cal, 0 g Fat, 0 g Sat Fat, 0 g Trans Fat, 0 mg Chol, 321 mg Sod, 35 g Carb, 4 g Fib, 7 g Prot, 131 mg Calc. **POINTS** value: **3.**

TIP To make yogurt cheese, spoon 1½ cups plain fat-free yogurt into a coffee filter or cheesecloth-lined strainer; place the strainer over a bowl. Refrigerate, covered, for at least 5 hours or overnight. Discard the liquid in the bowl. Makes ¾ cup yogurt cheese.

Italian Bread Salad

Sometimes known as Panzanella, this bread salad is great for using up day-old bread. Depending on how you like it, you can either serve the salad right away (while the bread is still chewy), or let it stand a few minutes before serving so that the bread has time to soften and soak up the flavors.

MAKES 4 SERVINGS

- 4 (½-inch-thick) day-old slices Tuscan or peasant bread, 3½ × 6 inches
- 2 tomatoes, coarsely chopped
- ½ cup thinly sliced cucumber
- ½ cup chopped scallions
- 2 tablespoons rinsed drained capers
- 2 tablespoons minced fresh basil
- 2 tablespoons red-wine vinegar
- 1 tablespoon + 1 teaspoon olive oil
- 1 garlic clove, minced
- ¼ teaspoon salt
- ¼ teaspoon freshly ground pepper

Spray the grill rack with nonstick spray; prepare the grill for a hot fire using the direct method (see page 81).

Place the bread slices on the grill rack and grill until crisp and browned, about 1½ minutes on each side. Transfer the bread to a cutting board and cut into ½-inch cubes.

Combine the grilled bread cubes, tomatoes, cucumber, scallions, capers, and basil in a large shallow serving bowl.

Combine the vinegar, oil, garlic, salt, and pepper in a small bowl. Drizzle the dressing over the bread mixture and toss gently to coat. Let stand about 3 minutes before serving.

PER SERVING (1 cup): 143 Cal, 6 g Fat, 1 g Sat Fat, 0 g Trans Fat, 0 mg Chol, 427 mg Sod, 20 g Carb, 2 g Fib, 4 g Prot, 51 mg Calc. *POINTS* value: *3.*

Pizzas and Breads

PIZZA GRILLING 101

If you've never tried grilled pizza before, you're in for a pleasant surprise. Once you taste one of these crisped and slightly smoky treats, you'll be hooked. Not only is the eating good, they are fun to make, especially if you enlist a friend or family member to help. Here are a few guidelines:

• Prevent the food or dough from sticking to the grill rack by scrubbing the rack clean of all debris before you begin, then spraying with nonstick spray.

• Prepare the grill for indirect cooking (see page 81). All our grilled pizzas require cooking over the direct heat section (directly above the heat source) of the grill, but they also require using the indirect section (the unheated side) of the grill while arranging the toppings on the pizzas.

• Have all the toppings and sauces you need to make the pizza prepared and assembled on a side table before grilling the crust.

• Place the rolled out pizza dough on a baking sheet (with no rim on at least one side) sprinkled with cornmeal. This will help the dough slide easily off the baking sheet onto the grill.

• Slide the pizza to the indirect cooking section for a minute or two if it browns too quickly. Tortillas, in particular, are thin, so check the bottoms frequently for over-browning and move to the cooler section of the grill, if necessary.

The Right Tools for the Job

For a successful and calm experience, it's important to set yourself up with everything you'll need before you get started. Here are the essentials:

• A covered grill. If you don't have one, improvise with a lid from a wok, an inverted metal bowl, or a tent of heavy-duty foil.

• Long-handled tongs and long oven mitts for dragging the pizza from one section of the grill to the other and to remove the pizza from the grill.

• A long-handled spatula or spoon for adding the toppings to the cooked pizza crust. Use the spatula or spoon to lightly press the toppings onto the crust.

• A grill basket with tightly spaced grids for grilling small toppings that would otherwise fall through the spaces on the grill rack.

• A side table to organize your toppings, sauces, tools, serving plates, and beverage of choice. Once you are well organized, you need only concern yourself with having a good time.

Basic Pizza Dough

This dough makes enough for two pizzas, so you can freeze half for another day. Thaw frozen dough in the refrigerator overnight, or on a counter for 1½ hours.

MAKES 2 (12-INCH) PIZZA CRUSTS (6 SERVINGS EACH CRUST)

1½ cups warm water (105°F–115°F)
  1 teaspoon sugar
  1 package active dry yeast
  1 tablespoon olive oil
4¼–4½ cups all-purpose flour
1½ teaspoons salt

Combine the water and sugar in a 2-cup measuring glass. Sprinkle in the yeast and let stand until foamy, about 5 minutes. Stir in the oil.

Combine the flour and salt in a food processor. With the machine running, scrape the yeast mixture through the feed tube; pulse until the dough forms a ball, about 1 minute. If necessary, turn the dough onto a lightly floured surface and knead briefly until smooth and elastic.

Spray a large bowl with nonstick spray; put the dough in the bowl. Cover lightly with plastic wrap and let rise in a warm place until double in size, about 1 hour.

Punch down the dough, then cut the dough in half. Refrigerate or freeze in floured zip-close freezer bags at this point or use as directed in the recipe.

PER SERVING (¹⁄₁₂ of dough): 174 Cal, 2 g Fat, 0 g Sat Fat, 0 g Trans Fat, 0 mg Chol, 292 mg Sod, 34 g Carb, 1 g Fib, 5 g Prot, 7 mg Calc. **POINTS** value: **3.**

VARIATIONS

Cornmeal Pizza Dough

Substitute 1 cup cornmeal for 1 cup of the all-purpose flour.

Per serving (¹⁄₁₂ of dough): 178 Cal, 2 g Fat, 0 g Sat Fat, 0 g Trans Fat, 0 mg Chol, 292 mg Sod, 35 g Carb, 2 g Fib, 5 g Prot, 6 mg Calc. **POINTS** value: **3.**

Whole-Wheat Pizza Dough

Substitute 1¼ cups whole-wheat flour for 1¼ cups of the all-purpose flour.

Per serving (¹⁄₁₂ of dough): 177 Cal, 2 g Fat, 0 g Sat Fat, 0 g Trans Fat, 0 mg Chol, 292 mg Sod, 34 g Carb, 3 g Fib, 6 g Prot, 5 mg Calc. **POINTS** value: **3.**

Pork and Poblano Pepper Pizza

This yields enough topping for two large or twelve small pizzas here.

MAKES 12 SERVINGS

3–4 tablespoons fresh lime juice
  2 large garlic cloves, crushed
  1 teaspoon dried oregano
  1 teaspoon ground cumin
  ½ teaspoon salt
  1 (1 pound) pork tenderloin
  6 poblano chile peppers
  1 cup crumbled feta cheese

  ½ cup shredded Monterey
     Jack cheese
  Cornmeal, for sprinkling
  1 recipe (about 2 pounds)
     Basic Pizza Dough (page 167),
     at room temperature
1¼ cups corn, fresh cut from the
     cob or frozen, thawed

Combine the lime juice, garlic, oregano, cumin, and salt in a zip-close plastic bag; add the pork. Seal the bag; turn to coat the pork. Refrigerate 1–2 hours.

Spray the grill rack with nonstick spray; prepare the grill for a medium fire using the indirect method (see page 81). Grill the pork over direct heat, turning as it browns, until an instant-read thermometer inserted into the thickest part of the pork registers 160°F for medium, 18–20 minutes. Wrap in foil; let stand 10 minutes, then thinly slice. Meanwhile, grill the peppers over direct heat, turning occasionally, until the skin blisters, about 12 minutes. Wrap in foil and let stand 15 minutes. Peel the peppers, discard the seeds, and cut into thin strips.

Combine the feta and Monterey Jack cheeses in a bowl. Sprinkle 2 large baking sheets with cornmeal. Knead the dough on a floured surface; cut in half or 12 pieces. Roll into 2 (12-inch) circles or 12 (4-inch) circles; transfer to the baking sheets, pulling the dough back into shape. Slide the crusts onto the direct-heat section of the grill. Cover the grill and cook until light grill marks form, 2–3 minutes.

Flip the crusts with tongs, then drag to the indirect-heat section of the grill. Sprinkle the cheeses over the crusts. Top evenly with the peppers, pork slices, then corn. Return half the pizzas to the direct-heat section of the grill. Cover the grill and cook until the toppings are hot and the bottoms are golden, 4–6 minutes for large pizzas, or 2–3 minutes for individual pizzas, switching the pizzas from the direct-heat of the grill to the indirect-heat section and vice versa once, so they cook evenly.

PER SERVING (⅙ of large pizza or 1 small pizza): 296 Cal, 7 g Fat, 4 g Sat Fat, 0 g Trans Fat, 40 mg Chol, 503 mg Sod, 40 g Carb, 2 g Fib, 17 g Prot, 109 mg Calc. **POINTS** value: **6.**

**PORK AND POBLANO
PEPPER PIZZA**

Steak Lovers' Grilled Pizza

Grilled flank steak (sliced very thin), onion (sliced quite thick) and a dab of herbed cheese make this a basic but excellent pizza topping.

MAKES 6 SERVINGS

 1 large garlic clove
 ¾ teaspoon salt
 ¼ teaspoon freshly ground pepper
 ½ pound flank steak
 2 medium onions, cut into
    ½-inch-thick slices
 1 large tomato, cut into
    ½-inch wedges

Cornmeal, for sprinkling
 ½ recipe (about 1 pound) Basic
    Pizza Dough (page 167),
    at room temperature
 ¼ cup light herb-seasoned soft
    spreading cheese

Chop the garlic, salt, and pepper to a paste on a board. Rub both sides of the steak with the paste. Place in a zip-close plastic bag and refrigerate, about 1 hour.

Spray grill rack with nonstick spray; prepare grill for a medium fire using indirect method (see page 81). Remove steak from bag; grill over direct heat, 4 minutes each side for medium-rare. Transfer steak to a board, let stand 5 minutes, then cut into thin slices.

Lightly spray onions with nonstick spray. Grill over direct heat until lightly charred and almost tender, 4–5 minutes on each side; wrap in foil, about 10 minutes. Grill the tomato wedges until light grill marks appear, about 1 minute.

Lightly sprinkle a large baking sheet with cornmeal. Sprinkle a work surface lightly with flour. Turn the dough onto surface; knead lightly. With a lightly floured rolling pin, roll into a 12-inch circle. Transfer circle to baking sheet, gently pulling dough back to a 12-inch circle. Slide crust onto direct-heat section of grill. Cover grill and cook until crust is firm and light grill marks are formed, 2–3 minutes.

Flip crust with tongs, then drag to the indirect-heat section of the grill. Quickly spread the cheese over the crust. Top evenly with the steak slices, onions, and tomato, leaving a ½-inch border. Return the pizza to the direct-heat section of the grill. Cover grill and cook until the toppings are hot and the bottom is golden, 3–5 minutes. Grab the edge of the pizza with tongs, then slide onto a board.

PER SERVING (⅙ of pizza): 278 Cal, 6 g Fat, 2 g Sat Fat, 0 g Trans Fat, 25 mg Chol, 662 mg Sod, 40 g Carb, 2 g Fib, 15 g Prot, 34 mg Calc. *POINTS* value: **6.**

Chicken, Corn, and Manchego Pizza

Grilled fresh corn on the cob adds color, crunch, and smoky flavor to this pizza.

MAKES 6 SERVINGS

1 teaspoon ground cumin

½ teaspoon onion powder

¾ teaspoon salt

¼ teaspoon freshly ground pepper

2 (4-ounce) skinless boneless chicken breast halves

2 ears fresh corn, shucked

1 small avocado, pitted and peeled

1 tablespoon fresh lime juice

½ teaspoon green hot pepper sauce (optional)

Cornmeal, for sprinkling

½ recipe (about 1 pound) Basic Pizza Dough—cornmeal variation (page 167), at room temperature

2 ounces manchego cheese, coarsely shredded (½ cup)

3 tablespoons finely chopped fresh cilantro

Spray the grill rack with nonstick spray; prepare the grill for a medium fire using the indirect method (see page 81). Combine the cumin, onion powder, ½ teaspoon of the salt, and the pepper in a cup. Sprinkle onto both sides of the chicken. Grill the chicken over direct heat until just cooked through, about 5 minutes on each side. Grill the corn alongside the chicken, turning as it chars, about 8 minutes. Slice the chicken. Cut the kernels off the cobs.

Mash the avocado, lime juice, pepper sauce (if using) and remaining ¼ teaspoon salt in a small bowl. Lightly sprinkle a large baking sheet with cornmeal. Turn the dough onto a lightly floured surface; knead lightly. With a floured rolling pin, roll into a 12-inch circle; transfer to the baking sheet, gently pulling the dough back to a 12-inch circle. Slide the crust onto the direct-heat section of the grill. Cover the grill and cook the crust until it is firm and light grill marks are formed, 2-3 minutes.

Flip the crust with tongs, then drag to the indirect-heat section of the grill. Quickly spread the avocado mixture over the crust. Top evenly with the chicken slices, corn, cheese, and cilantro, leaving a ½-inch border. Return the pizza to the direct-heat section of the grill. Cover grill and cook until toppings are hot and bottom is golden, 3-5 minutes. Grab edge of pizza with tongs, then slide onto a board.

PER SERVING (⅙ of pizza): 331 Cal, 10 g Fat, 3 g Sat Fat, 0 g Trans Fat, 29 mg Chol, 704 mg Sod, 45 g Carb, 4 g Fib, 17 g Prot, 89 mg Calc. *POINTS* value: *7.*

Sage Chicken and Pepper Pizza

Fresh sage, chicken, and colorful bell peppers make a great pizza topping here.

MAKES 6 SERVINGS

4 (4-ounce) skinless boneless
  chicken thighs
2 tablespoons finely chopped
  fresh sage
2 large garlic cloves,
  finely chopped
1 teaspoon salt
1 large yellow bell pepper,
  halved and seeded

1 large red bell pepper,
  halved and seeded
Cornmeal, for sprinkling
½ recipe (about 1 pound) Basic
  Pizza Dough—cornmeal
  variation (page 167),
  at room temperature
⅓ cup part-skim shredded
  mozzarella cheese

Combine the chicken, sage, garlic, and ½ teaspoon of the salt in a zip-close plastic bag; rub the seasonings onto the chicken by pressing on the outside of the bag. Squeeze out the air and seal the bag; refrigerate 1 hour.

Spray the grill rack with nonstick spray; prepare the grill for a medium fire using indirect method (see page 81). Grill peppers over direct heat until lightly charred and tender, 8–10 minutes on each side. Wrap in foil and let stand until cool enough to handle, about 15 minutes. Peel and cut into ½-inch strips; toss with remaining ½ teaspoon salt. Meanwhile, remove chicken from bag, then grill over direct heat until cooked through, 4–5 minutes on each side. Coarsely chop chicken.

Lightly sprinkle a large baking sheet with cornmeal. Turn the dough onto a lightly floured surface; knead lightly. With a floured rolling pin, roll into a 12-inch circle; transfer to the baking sheet, gently pulling the dough back to a 12-inch circle. Slide the crust onto the direct-heat section of the grill. Cover the grill and cook the crust until it is firm and light grill marks are formed, 2–3 minutes.

Flip the crust with tongs, then drag to the indirect-heat section of the grill. Sprinkle the cheese over the crust. Top evenly with the peppers and chicken. Return the pizza to the direct-heat section of the grill. Cover the grill and cook until the toppings are hot and the bottom is golden, 3–5 minutes. Grab the edge of the pizza with tongs, then slide onto a board.

PER SERVING (⅙ of pizza): 325 Cal, 8 g Fat, 2 g Sat Fat, 0 g Trans Fat, 54 mg Chol, 763 mg Sod, 39 g Carb, 3 g Fib, 23 g Prot, 75 mg Calc. *POINTS* value: *7.*

Herbed Duck and Tomato Pizza

MAKES 6 SERVINGS

2 tablespoons balsamic vinegar

1½ teaspoons packed brown sugar

1 teaspoon minced rosemary

1 large garlic clove, crushed

½ teaspoon salt

1 (¾-pound) skinless boneless duck breast half

1 large red onion, cut crosswise into ¼-inch slices

2 medium plum tomatoes, diced

Cornmeal, for sprinkling

½ recipe (about 1 pound) Basic Pizza Dough (page 167), at room temperature

¼ cup shredded part-skim mozzarella cheese

2 tablespoons lightly packed, thinly sliced basil leaves

½ cup crumbled goat cheese

10 kalamata olives, sliced

Combine the vinegar, sugar, rosemary, garlic, and salt in a zip-close plastic bag; transfer 1½ teaspoons of the mixture to a small bowl. Add the duck to the bag. Squeeze out the air and seal the bag; turn to coat the duck. Refrigerate, turning the bag occasionally, 3–4 hours. Cover the reserved marinade and set aside.

Spray the grill rack with nonstick spray; prepare the grill for a medium fire using the indirect method (see page 81). Remove the duck from the bag and grill with the onion over direct heat until the duck is browned with grill marks and the onion is tender, 3–4 minutes on each side (medium-rare for the duck). Wrap the onion in foil; let stand 10 minutes. Cut the duck into thin slices. Toss the tomatoes with the reserved marinade in the small bowl.

Lightly sprinkle a large baking sheet with cornmeal. Turn the dough onto a lightly floured surface; knead lightly. With a floured rolling pin, roll into a 12-inch circle; transfer to the baking sheet, gently pulling the dough back to a 12-inch circle. Slide the crust onto the direct-heat section of the grill. Cover the grill and cook the crust until it is firm and light grill marks are formed, 2–3 minutes.

Flip the crust with tongs, then drag to indirect-heat section of the grill. Sprinkle the mozzarella over the crust. Top evenly with the duck and onion, separating the rings. Sprinkle with the basil, tomatoes, goat cheese, and olives. Return pizza to direct-heat section of grill. Cover grill and cook until toppings are hot and bottom is golden, 3–5 minutes. Grab edge of pizza with tongs, then slide onto a board.

PER SERVING (⅙ of pizza): 336 Cal, 10 g Fat, 4 g Sat Fat, 0 g Trans Fat, 51 mg Chol, 527 mg Sod, 39 g Carb, 2 g Fib, 22 g Prot, 138 mg Calc. ***POINTS*** value: *7.*

SMOKED TURKEY, GRILLED
ONION, AND TOMATO PIZZA

Smoked Turkey, Grilled Onion, and Tomato Pizza

Tex-Mex flavors dominate in this simple, smoky pizza—filled with grilled sweet onion and scallions, mesquite-flavored turkey, and melted Swiss cheese.

MAKES 6 SERVINGS

1 large sweet onion, cut into scant ½-inch-thick slices
1 bunch scallions, trimmed
Cornmeal, for sprinkling
½ recipe (about 1 pound) Basic Pizza Dough—whole-wheat variation (page 167), at room temperature

⅔ cup shredded low-fat Swiss or Gruyère cheese
¼ pound mesquite-flavored sliced smoked turkey breast, chopped
1 cup diced tomato

Spray the grill rack with nonstick spray; prepare the grill for a medium fire using the indirect method (see page 81). Lightly spray the sweet onion and scallions with nonstick spray. Grill the sweet onion slices over direct heat until lightly charred and almost tender, 4–5 minutes on each side. Wrap in foil to steam and help tenderize them, about 10 minutes. Grill the scallions until charred, 2–3 minutes; cut into approximately 1-inch pieces.

Lightly sprinkle a large baking sheet with cornmeal. Sprinkle a work surface lightly with flour. Turn the dough onto the surface; knead lightly. With a lightly floured rolling pin, roll into a 12-inch circle. Transfer the circle of dough to the baking sheet, gently pulling the dough back to a 12-inch circle. Slide the crust from the baking sheet onto the direct-heat section of the grill. Cover the grill and cook the crust until it is firm and light grill marks are formed, 2–3 minutes.

Flip the crust with tongs, then drag to the indirect-heat section of the grill. Quickly sprinkle ⅓ cup of the cheese over the crust. Top evenly with the onion, scallions, turkey, tomato, and the remaining ⅓ cup cheese, leaving a ½-inch border. Return the pizza to the direct-heat section of the grill. Cover the grill and cook until the toppings are hot and the bottom is golden, 3–5 minutes. Grab the edge of the pizza with tongs, then slide onto a board.

PER SERVING (⅙ of pizza): 252 Cal, 4 g Fat, 1 g Sat Fat, 0 g Trans Fat, 12 mg Chol, 622 mg Sod, 42 g Carb, 4 g Fib, 14 g Prot, 133 mg Calc. *POINTS* value: **5.**

California Sausage-and-Pepper Pizza

Gourmet-flavored chicken or duck sausage, bright yellow bell peppers, and creamy goat cheese make up this strictly California take on sausage-and-pepper pizza.

MAKES 6 SERVINGS

2 large yellow bell peppers, cut in half lengthwise and seeded
1 large red onion, cut in half lengthwise
2 links (½ pound) low-fat chicken or duck sausage, preferably with Southwestern flavors
1½ teaspoons olive oil
1½ teaspoons white balsamic vinegar
¼ teaspoon salt
Cornmeal, for sprinkling
½ recipe (about 1 pound) Basic Pizza Dough (page 167), at room temperature
½ cup crumbled goat cheese, at room temperature

Spray the grill rack with nonstick spray; prepare the grill for a medium fire using the indirect method (see page 81). Lightly spray the bell peppers and onion with nonstick spray. Grill the bell peppers over direct heat until tender and the skin is charred, 8–10 minutes on each side. Wrap in foil and let stand until cool enough to handle, about 15 minutes. Grill the onion and sausage over direct heat until lightly charred, about 10 minutes, turning as they brown. Peel the peppers and cut into ½-inch strips. Cut the onion into wedges, pull apart and toss with the peppers, oil, vinegar, and salt in a large bowl. Slice the sausage on a diagonal.

Lightly sprinkle a large baking sheet with cornmeal. Turn the dough onto a lightly floured surface; knead lightly. With a floured rolling pin, roll into a 12-inch circle; transfer to the baking sheet, gently pulling the dough back to a 12-inch circle. Slide the crust onto the direct-heat section of the grill. Cover the grill and cook the crust until it is firm and light grill marks are formed, 2–3 minutes.

Flip the crust with tongs, then drag to the indirect-heat section of the grill. Top evenly with the pepper mixture and sausage, leaving a ½-inch border. Sprinkle with the goat cheese. Return the pizza to the direct-heat section of the grill. Cover the grill and cook until the toppings are hot and the bottom is golden, 3–5 minutes. Grab the edge of the pizza with tongs, then slide onto a board.

PER SERVING (⅙ of pizza): 292 Cal, 7 g Fat, 3 g Sat Fat, 0 g Trans Fat, 26 mg Chol, 752 mg Sod, 45 g Carb, 3 g Fib, 13 g Prot, 85 mg Calc. *POINTS* value: **6.**

CALIFORNIA
SAUSAGE-AND-PEPPER
PIZZA

Grilled Canadian Bacon and Pear Pizza

Pear and smoked ham on whole-wheat bread has been a trendy sandwich in upscale delis and cafés for several years now. This pizza—essentially an open-face grilled sandwich—takes this delicious pairing to new, easy culinary heights.

MAKES 6 SERVINGS

- 2 tablespoons fresh lime juice
- 2 teaspoons honey
- 2 firm-ripe pears, peeled, halved lengthwise, and cored
- 2 tablespoons diced red onion
- 1 teaspoon minced fresh thyme
- ½ pound Canadian bacon slices
- Cornmeal, for sprinkling

- ½ recipe (about 1 pound) Basic Pizza Dough-whole-wheat variation (page 167), at room temperature
- ⅔ cup reduced-fat Gruyère or Gouda cheese
- ⅔ cup lightly packed baby spinach leaves

Spray the grill rack with nonstick spray; prepare the grill for a medium fire using the indirect method (see page 81). Combine the lime juice and honey in a medium bowl. Add the pears and toss to coat; remove the pears and set aside. Add the onion and thyme to the lime juice mixture; set aside. Grill the pears and the bacon over direct heat until grill marks appear and the bacon is hot, 1½–2 minutes on each side. Cut the pear into ½-inch dice and slice the bacon into strips.

Lightly sprinkle a large baking sheet with cornmeal. Sprinkle a work surface lightly with flour. Turn the dough onto the surface; knead lightly. With a lightly floured rolling pin, roll into a 12-inch circle. Transfer the circle of dough to the baking sheet, gently pulling the dough back to a 12-inch circle. Slide the crust from the baking sheet onto the direct-heat section of the grill. Cover the grill and cook the crust until it is firm and light grill marks are formed, 2–3 minutes.

Flip the crust with tongs, then drag to the indirect-heat section of the grill. Quickly sprinkle ⅓ cup of the cheese over the crust. Top evenly with the bacon, spinach, and pears and the remaining ⅓ cup cheese, leaving a ½-inch border. Return the pizza to the direct-heat section of the grill. Cover the grill and cook until the toppings are hot and the bottom is golden, 3–5 minutes. Grab the edge of the pizza with tongs, then slide onto a board.

PER SERVING (⅙ of pizza): 302 Cal, 6 g Fat, 2 g Sat Fat, 0 g Trans Fat, 22 mg Chol, 502 mg Sod, 46 g Carb, 4 g Fib, 17 g Prot, 176 mg Calc. **POINTS** value: *6*

Coastal Pizza

Fresh salmon, scallions, lemon, and thyme make this a pizza fit for any mariner.

MAKES 6 SERVINGS

- 3 tablespoons fresh lemon juice
- 1½ teaspoons minced fresh thyme
- ¾ teaspoon salt
- 1 teaspoon extra-virgin olive oil
- ⅛ teaspoon freshly ground pepper
- ½ pound center-cut salmon fillet with skin
- 2 bunches scallions, trimmed
- 1 cup lightly packed coarsely chopped frisee
- Cornmeal, for sprinkling
- ½ recipe (about 1 pound) Basic Pizza Dough—cornmeal variation (page 167), at room temperature
- ½ cup crumbled reduced-fat goat cheese

Spray the grill rack with nonstick spray; prepare the grill for a medium fire using the indirect method (see page 81). Combine the lemon juice, thyme, and ½ teaspoon of the salt in a large shallow dish. Transfer 1 tablespoon of the mixture to a medium bowl; add oil, remaining ¼ teaspoon salt, and pepper. Set aside. Add salmon to the large dish and turn to coat; let stand 15 minutes.

Lightly spray the salmon and scallions with nonstick spray. Grill the salmon over direct heat until opaque in the center and lightly charred on the outside, about 4 minutes on each side. Discard the skin. Break the salmon into large flakes. Grill the scallions until lightly charred, 2–3 minutes; cut into approximately 1-inch pieces. Toss the frisée with the reserved dressing in the bowl.

Lightly sprinkle a large baking sheet with cornmeal. Turn the dough onto a lightly floured surface; knead lightly. With a floured rolling pin, roll into a 12-inch circle; transfer to the baking sheet, gently pulling the dough back to a 12-inch circle. Slide the crust onto the direct-heat section of the grill. Cover the grill and cook the crust until it is firm and light grill marks are formed, 2–3 minutes.

Flip the crust with tongs, then drag to the indirect-heat section of the grill. Quickly spread the cheese over the crust. Top evenly with the frisée, then the salmon and scallions, leaving a ½-inch border. Return the pizza to the direct-heat section of grill. Cover grill and cook until toppings are hot and bottom is golden, 3–5 minutes. Grab the edge of the pizza with tongs, then slide onto a board.

PER SERVING (⅙ of pizza): 283 Cal, 6 g Fat, 2 g Sat Fat, 0 g Trans Fat, 36 mg Chol, 562 mg Sod, 41 g Carb, 4 g Fib, 16 g Prot, 120 mg Calc. **POINTS** value: **5.**

Grilled Radicchio and Shiitake Pizza

MAKES 6 SERVINGS

½ cup fat-free balsamic vinaigrette

2 garlic cloves, crushed

1 tablespoon whole-grain honey mustard

½ teaspoon chopped fresh rosemary

½ teaspoon salt

1½ teaspoons olive oil

3 medium plum tomatoes, thinly sliced

½ pound fresh shiitake mushrooms, stems removed

1 large (6-ounce) head radicchio lettuce, cut in half through the core

Cornmeal, for sprinkling

½ recipe (about 1 pound) Basic Pizza Dough—cornmeal variation (page 167), at room temperature

½ cup shredded Gruyère cheese

Combine the vinaigrette, garlic, mustard, rosemary, and salt in a large bowl; transfer 1½ teaspoons to a large shallow plate. Add the oil to plate. Add tomatoes, turn to coat. Add the mushrooms and radicchio to the remaining vinaigrette mixture in the large bowl; turn to coat and let stand 30 minutes.

Spray the grill rack with nonstick spray; prepare the grill for a medium fire using the indirect method (see page 81). Spray a grill basket with nonstick spray; add mushrooms. Grill over direct heat, turning occasionally, until tender and lightly browned, 8–10 minutes. Place radicchio alongside basket and grill until collapsed and browned, 4–5 minutes on each side; transfer radicchio to a board and slice.

Lightly sprinkle a large baking sheet with cornmeal. Turn dough onto floured surface. With floured rolling pin, roll to 12-inch circle; transfer to baking sheet, pulling dough back to 12-inch circle. Slide crust onto direct-heat section of grill. Cover grill and cook crust until firm and light grill marks are formed, 2–3 minutes.

Flip the crust with tongs, then drag to the indirect-heat section of grill. Sprinkle cheese over crust. Top evenly with the mushrooms and radicchio, leaving a ½-inch border. Return pizza to direct-heat section of grill. Cover grill and cook until toppings are hot and bottom is golden, 3–5 minutes. Grab edge of pizza with tongs, then slide onto a board. Top cooked pizza with marinated tomato slices.

PER SERVING (⅙ of pizza): 251 Cal, 6 g Fat, 2 g Sat Fat, 0 g Trans Fat, 9 mg Chol, 425 mg Sod, 41 g Carb, 3 g Fib, 9 g Prot, 108 mg Calc. *POINTS* value: *5.*

Spicy Sausage and White Bean Pizza

Hot Italian sausage gives a nice kick to this simple pizza, but you can use sweet Italian sausage or any flavored low-fat turkey, chicken, or duck sausage.

MAKES 6 SERVINGS 🔥

- 2 links (½ pound) low-fat hot Italian turkey sausage
- 4 plum tomatoes, cut in half lengthwise
- 1 (10-ounce) thin prebaked pizza crust
- ⅔ cup shredded part-skim mozzarella cheese
- 1 cup canned cannellini (white kidney) beans, rinsed and drained

Spray the grill rack with nonstick spray; prepare the grill for a medium fire using the direct method (see page 81). Place the sausage on the grill rack; cover the grill. Grill until cooked through, turning as it browns, about 15 minutes. Lightly spray the tomatoes with nonstick spray, then grill, skin-side down, until the skin is just lightly charred, 2–3 minutes. Transfer the tomatoes to a plate and set aside. Slice the sausage on a slight diagonal; set aside.

Place the crust, top-side down, on the grill; cover the grill. Grill until the crust is lightly crisped and golden, 2–3 minutes. Flip the crust with tongs, then sprinkle evenly with ⅓ cup of the cheese. Arrange the sausage and tomatoes on the crust. Scatter the beans on top, then sprinkle with the remaining ⅓ cup cheese. Cover the grill and cook until the toppings are heated through and the crust is deep golden, 2–4 minutes. Grab edge of pizza with tongs, then slide onto a board.

PER SERVING (⅙ of pizza): 262 Cal, 6 g Fat, 2 g Sat Fat, 0 g Trans Fat, 21 mg Chol, 678 mg Sod, 36 g Carb, 3 g Fib, 16 g Prot, 130 mg Calc. **POINTS** value: **5.**

TIP Be aware that many chicken or duck sausages are fully cooked and only need to be grilled until heated through and grill marks are formed, about 4 minutes on each side.

SPANISH TORTILLA PIZZA

Spanish Tortilla Pizza

Serrano ham, a Spanish ham that's air-dried, often with paprika, is similar to prosciutto. Both are usually served in thin slices and a little packs a lot of flavor. Manchego cheese is the most popular sheep's milk cheese in Spain and, like serrano ham, is full of flavor. The 9- to 10-inch flour tortillas are often referred to as burrito-size tortillas.

MAKES 6 SERVINGS

2 large red bell peppers, cut in half lengthwise and seeded

1 teaspoon olive oil

1/8 teaspoon saffron threads

1 teaspoon sherry vinegar

1 teaspoon nonpareil capers

3 (9- to 10-inch) whole-wheat or regular flour tortillas

2 ounces manchego cheese, coarsely shredded (1/2 cup)

2 ounces sliced serrano or prosciutto ham, cut into strips

Spray the grill rack with nonstick spray; prepare the grill for a medium fire using the direct method (see page 81). Lightly spray the bell peppers with nonstick spray. Grill until tender and the skin is charred, 8–10 minutes on each side. Wrap in foil and let stand until cool enough to handle, about 15 minutes.

Meanwhile, microwave the oil and saffron in a microwavable large bowl on High until very warm, 30–40 seconds. With a fork, whisk in the vinegar and capers. Peel and cut the bell peppers into 1/2-inch strips. Add the peppers to the saffron vinaigrette and toss together.

Place the tortillas on the grill rack. Grill until lightly crisped and golden on the bottom, 1–2 minutes. Flip the tortillas with tongs. Scatter the peppers evenly on the tortillas, then sprinkle with the cheese and ham. Cover the grill and cook until the cheese melts and the bottom is lightly crisped, 1–3 minutes. Cut each tortilla into fourths, making a total of 12 pieces.

PER SERVING (2 pieces): 112 Cal, 5 g Fat, 2 g Sat Fat, 0 g Trans Fat, 14 mg Chol, 341 mg Sod, 11 g Carb, 2 g Fib, 6 g Prot, 78 mg Calc. *POINTS* value: *2.*

TIP The peppers can be grilled ahead of time and refrigerated without the dressing in a zip-close plastic bag for up to 4 days. Bring to room temperature and toss with the dressing before topping the tortillas.

Zucchini and Goat Cheese on Flatbread

Flatbreads make quick and delicious alternatives to traditional pizza crusts. Here we use nan—an elongated oval Indian flatbread, similar to a pocketless pita bread. Onion flatbread makes a flavorful alternative to the plain flatbread, if you can find it.

MAKES 6 SERVINGS

3 tablespoons fresh lemon juice

2–3 garlic cloves, crushed

1½ teaspoons olive oil

1½ teaspoons minced fresh thyme

½ teaspoon salt

2 medium zucchini, cut in half crosswise, then cut into ¼-inch-thick slices, lengthwise

3 (9 × 3½-inch) oval nan flatbreads

½ cup crumbled goat cheese, at room temperature

Combine the lemon juice, garlic, oil, thyme, and salt in a zip-close plastic bag; add the zucchini. Squeeze out the air and seal the bag; turn to coat the zucchini. Let stand 30 minutes.

Spray the grill rack with nonstick spray; prepare the grill for a medium fire using the direct method (see page 81). Remove the zucchini from the plastic bag and place on the grill rack. Grill until tender and grill marks appear, 3–4 minutes on each side. Transfer the zucchini to a plate and set aside.

Place the flatbreads on the grill rack and grill until lightly crisped and golden on the bottom, 2–3 minutes. Flip with tongs, then evenly sprinkle the cheese on the flatbreads. Arrange the zucchini on top in slightly overlapping rows and press down lightly. Cover the grill and cook until the bottoms of the flatbreads are lightly crisped, about 3 minutes. Cut each flatbread in half crosswise, making a total of 6 pieces.

PER SERVING (1 piece): 162 Cal, 4 g Fat, 2 g Sat Fat, 0 g Trans Fat, 11 mg Chol, 319 mg Sod, 26 g Carb, 2 g Fib, 6 g Prot, 109 mg Calc. *POINTS* value: **3.**

ZUCCHINI AND GOAT
CHEESE ON FLATBREAD

Shrimp, Hummus, and Red Pepper Pizza

Great for patio parties, this bruschetta-style grilled pizza also makes great appetizers when you cut each serving into quarters. To save time, buy the shrimp already peeled and deveined.

MAKES 4 SERVINGS

- **2 medium red bell peppers, cut in half lengthwise and seeded**
- **2 tablespoons thinly sliced fresh basil leaves**
- **½ teaspoon ground cumin**
- **¼ teaspoon salt**
- **¼ teaspoon cayenne (optional)**

- **½ pound large shrimp, peeled and deveined**
- **4 (½-inch-thick) slices Tuscan or peasant bread, 3½ × 6 inches**
- **½ cup 40-spice or regular hummus**

Spray the grill rack with nonstick spray; prepare the grill for a medium fire using the direct method (see page 81). Lightly spray the bell peppers with nonstick spray. Place the peppers on the grill. Grill until tender and the skin is charred, 8–10 minutes on each side. Wrap in foil and let stand until cool enough to handle, about 15 minutes. Peel the peppers, cut into ¼-inch strips, and toss with the basil.

Meanwhile, combine the cumin, salt, and cayenne, if using, on a sheet of wax paper. Sprinkle the shrimp with the spices, working over the wax paper. Place the shrimp on the grill rack. Grill until golden on the outside and opaque in the center, 2–3 minutes. Transfer to a cutting board to cool slightly, then chop.

Place the bread on the grill rack and grill just until lightly toasted and crisped, about 1 minute on each side. Spread the hummus evenly on one side of each of the toasts. Top with the bell pepper mixture, then the shrimp. Serve at once.

PER SERVING (1 toast): 195 Cal, 5 g Fat, 1 g Sat Fat, 0 g Trans Fat, 53 mg Chol, 549 mg Sod, 26 g Carb, 4 g Fib, 12 g Prot, 78 mg Calc. **POINTS** value: **4.**

TIP To peel and devein shrimp, first remove the shells and tails. Lay the shrimp on a board. Using a sharp paring knife, slice along the back of the shrimp from top to tail, cutting into the shrimp about ⅛ inch. Scrape out the vein with the knife blade and rinse under cold running water.

Grilled Eggplant and Feta Pitas

Eggplant and feta cheese, a traditional Greek pairing, are delicious seasoned with garlic and oregano and grilled on pocketless pita breads.

MAKES 6 SERVINGS

¼ cup balsamic vinegar

2 large garlic cloves, crushed

1½ teaspoons olive oil

1 teaspoon dried oregano

½ teaspoon salt

¼ teaspoon sugar

1 (1¼-pound) eggplant, cut into 12 rounds

3 (6 to 7-inch) pocketless pita breads

¾ cup crumbled feta cheese

Combine the vinegar, garlic, oil, oregano, salt, and sugar in a zip-close plastic bag; add the eggplant. Squeeze out the air and seal the bag; turn to coat the eggplant. Let stand 1 hour.

Spray the grill rack with nonstick spray; prepare the grill for a medium fire using the direct method (see page 81). Remove the eggplant from the plastic bag and arrange on the grill. Cover the grill and cook the eggplant until tender and charred in spots with grill marks, about 6 minutes on each side. Wrap the eggplant in foil and let stand 15 minutes.

Place the pita breads on the grill rack and grill until lightly crisped and golden on the bottom, 2–3 minutes. Flip with tongs, then arrange the eggplant slices evenly on top. Sprinkle evenly with the cheese. Cover the grill and cook until the cheese melts slightly and the breads are lightly crisped, about 3 minutes. Cut each pita in half crosswise, making a total of 6 pieces.

PER SERVING (1 piece): 148 Cal, 5 g Fat, 3 g Sat Fat, 0 g Trans Fat, 17 mg Chol, 396 mg Sod, 21 g Carb, 3 g Fib, 6 g Prot, 121 mg Calc. *POINTS* value: *3.*

TIP Don't skip wrapping the grilled eggplant in foil—the trapped heat creates steam, which helps to tenderize the eggplant.

Pita Breads with Thyme

Homemade pitas are a cinch—just remember to prepare the dough a few hours ahead so the pitas are ready to pop on the grill at just the right moment.

MAKES 8 SERVINGS

1 cup warm (105°F – 115°F) water
¼ teaspoon sugar
1 package active dry yeast
1 tablespoon olive oil
2½ cups all-purpose flour
½ cup whole-wheat flour
2 teaspoons salt
1 teaspoon dried thyme or rosemary leaves, crumbled
½ teaspoon freshly ground pepper

Combine the water and sugar in a 2-cup measuring glass. Sprinkle in the yeast and let stand until foamy, about 5 minutes. Stir in the oil.

Combine the all-purpose and whole-wheat flours, the salt, thyme, and pepper in a food processor. With the machine running, scrape the yeast mixture through the feed tube; pulse until the dough forms a ball, about 1 minute. If necessary, turn the dough onto a lightly floured surface and knead briefly until smooth and elastic.

Spray a large bowl with nonstick spray; place the dough in the bowl. Cover loosely with plastic wrap and let the dough rise in a warm place until it doubles in size, about 1 hour.

Punch down the dough; let it stand about 10 minutes. Divide the dough into 8 equal pieces, forming each piece into a ball. Cover the dough balls loosely with plastic wrap and let stand about 30 minutes.

Spray the grill rack with nonstick spray; prepare the grill for a medium fire using the direct method (see page 81).

Roll or pat out each ball to slightly less than ⅛-inch thickness. Cover with plastic wrap and let stand about 30 minutes.

Using a spatula, transfer the pitas to the edge of the grill. Grill until the pitas are puffed with brown spots on the bottom, 3–4 minutes. Turn and grill 3–4 minutes more. Remove the pitas from the grill and wrap in foil at once so that the breads stay moist; they will deflate as they cool.

PER SERVING (1 pita): 188 Cal, 2 g Fat, 0 g Sat Fat, 0 g Trans Fat, 0 mg Chol, 552 mg Sod, 36 g Carb, 2 g Fib, 5 g Prot, 20 mg Calc. *POINTS* value: *4.*

Colonial Spoon Bread

Rice bread has been an American staple since Colonial times, especially in the Carolinas where rice was first cultivated. This is an interesting variation of the usual Southern all-cornmeal spoon bread. It comes out golden and crisp at the edges and fairly firm in the center. It can be made ahead of time and reheated.

MAKES 8 SERVINGS

- 1 **cup cooked long-grain white rice**
- ¼ **cup cornmeal**
- 1 **cup plain low-fat yogurt**
- 1 **cup evaporated fat-free milk**
- ¾ **teaspoon salt**
- ½ **teaspoon baking soda**
- ¼ **cup fat-free egg substitute**
- 1 **egg, lightly beaten**
- 1 **tablespoon butter, melted**

Prepare the grill for a medium-hot fire using the direct method (see page 81). Spray a 9-inch cast-iron skillet with nonstick spray.

Combine the rice, cornmeal, yogurt, milk, salt, baking soda, egg substitute, egg, and butter in a medium bowl, whisking just until blended.

Spread the rice mixture evenly into the skillet. Place the skillet on the top rack of the grill or at least 10–12 inches from the heat. Close the grill cover or tent the skillet with foil. Bake until the bread is crusty and a toothpick inserted in the center comes out clean, about 25 minutes. Cut into 8 wedges and serve hot.

PER SERVING (1 wedge): 118 Cal, 3 g Fat, 1 g Sat Fat, 0 g Trans Fat, 33 mg Chol, 376 mg Sod, 16 g Carb, 0 g Fib, 6 g Prot, 155 mg Calc. *POINTS* value: *3.*

Southern Corn Bread in a Skillet

Corn bread cooked in a cast-iron skillet has been a part of American cuisine for many years, especially in the South. This easy-to-prepare quick bread can be "baking" on the top grill rack as you cook dinner on the rest of the grill.

MAKES 8 SERVINGS

1¼ cups all-purpose flour

¾ cup cornmeal

¼ cup sugar

2 teaspoons baking powder

1 cup fat-free milk

1 egg

2 tablespoons canola oil

Prepare the grill for a hot fire using the direct method (see page 81). Spray a 10-inch cast-iron skillet with nonstick spray.

Combine the flour, cornmeal, sugar, and baking powder in a large bowl. Stir in the milk, egg, and oil; mix just until the dry ingredients are thoroughly moistened.

Pour the batter into the skillet; place the skillet on the top rack of the grill or at least 10–12 inches from the heat. Close the grill cover or tent the skillet with foil. Bake until golden and a toothpick inserted in the center comes out clean, about 15 minutes. Cut into 8 wedges and serve hot.

PER SERVING (1 wedge): 194 Cal, 5 g Fat, 1 g Sat Fat, 0 g Trans Fat, 27 mg Chol, 147 mg Sod, 33 g Carb, 1 g Fib, 5 g Prot, 112 mg Calc. *POINTS* value: *4.*

Marinades, Sauces, Relishes, and Toppings

Asian-Style Marinade

For a piquant sweet-and-sour flavor, brush this marinade on poultry, pork, or even vegetables as they grill.

MAKES 4 SERVINGS

- ½ cup reduced-sodium chicken broth
- 3 tablespoons rice-wine vinegar
- 4 garlic cloves, minced
- 2 tablespoons reduced-sodium soy sauce
- 1 tablespoon + 1 teaspoon dark molasses
- 1 teaspoon Asian (dark) sesame oil
- ¼ teaspoon crushed red pepper

Whisk together broth, vinegar, garlic, soy sauce, molasses, oil, and crushed red pepper in medium bowl. Cover and refrigerate until ready to use, up to 1 day.

PER SERVING (¼ cup): 55 Cal, 1 g Fat, 0 g Sat Fat, 0 g Trans Fat, 0 mg Chol, 279 mg Sod, 10 g Carb, 0 g Fib, 2 g Prot, 34 mg Calc. *POINTS* value: *1.*

TIP Available in most grocery stores, Asian (dark) sesame oil adds an intense sesame flavor that is integral to this marinade. If you substitute regular sesame oil or vegetable oil, the flavor will be very different.

Rosemary and Lemon Marinade

This delicate recipe adds powerful flavor to white meat chicken. Use it as a tenderizing marinade, or brush it onto poultry as it grills. One batch is perfect for about 1 pound of skinless, boneless chicken.

MAKES 4 SERVINGS

¼ cup hot water
¾ teaspoon dried rosemary, crumbled
½ teaspoon grated lemon zest
2 tablespoons fresh lemon juice

2 teaspoons olive oil
1 garlic clove, minced
½ teaspoon salt
⅛ teaspoon freshly ground pepper

Pour the hot water over the rosemary leaves in a glass jar or glass measuring cup; let cool. Stir in the lemon zest, lemon juice, oil, garlic, salt, and pepper. Cover and refrigerate until ready to use, up to 1 week.

PER SERVING (1 tablespoon): 24 Cal, 2 g Fat, 0 g Sat Fat, 0 g Trans Fat, 1 mg Chol, 297 mg Sod, 1 g Carb, 0 g Fib, 0 g Prot, 6 mg Calc. *POINTS* value: *1.*

TIP The zest of the lemon is the peel without any of the pith (white membrane). To remove the zest from a lemon, use a zester or the fine side of a box grater.

 Creamy Cilantro Marinade

Here's a simple marinade that tenderizes and flavors chicken and lamb, and tastes especially delicious with fish. The recipe makes about 1 cup marinade, enough for about 1 pound of poultry, meat, or fish.

MAKES 4 SERVINGS

¾ cup plain fat-free yogurt

2 tablespoons minced fresh cilantro

2 tablespoons fresh lime juice

1 tablespoon + 1 teaspoon canola oil

1 teaspoon Dijon mustard

1 garlic clove, minced

Combine the yogurt, cilantro, lime juice, oil, mustard, and garlic in a medium bowl. Cover and refrigerate until ready to use, up to 1 day.

PER SERVING (¼ cup): 70 Cal, 5 g Fat, 1 g Sat Fat, 0 g Trans Fat, 1 mg Chol, 68 mg Sod, 4 g Carb, 0 g Fib, 3 g Prot, 95 mg Calc. *POINTS* value: *2.*

MARINATING NOTES

Marinades tenderize and add rich flavor—with little if any fat—to meats poultry, fish, and vegetables to be grilled. The right marinade can turn a tough cut of lean meat or a mild-flavored vegetable into something juicy and wonderful. Larger cuts of meat take longer to marinate, often overnight; fish, small pieces of poultry, and vegetables can take as little as 10 minutes.

☑ Spicy Mint and Cumin Rub

To enjoy the wonderful flavors of North Africa, rub this spicy mixture on a pound of chicken, fish, or any meat, cover and refrigerate it for about 1 hour, then grill.

MAKES 4 SERVINGS

- ¼ cup minced fresh parsley
- 2 tablespoons + 2 teaspoons fresh lemon juice
- 2 teaspoons paprika
- 2 teaspoons minced fresh mint
- 1 teaspoon ground cumin
- 2 garlic cloves, minced
- 1 teaspoon extra-virgin olive oil
- ½ teaspoon salt
- ¼ teaspoon cayenne

Combine the parsley, lemon juice, paprika, mint, cumin, garlic, oil, salt, and cayenne; mix well. Cover and refrigerate until ready to use, up to 1 day.

PER SERVING (1 tablespoon): 21 Cal, 1 g Fat, 0 g Sat Fat, 0 g Trans Fat, 0 mg Chol, 301 mg Sod, 2 g Carb, 1 g Fib, 1 g Prot, 17 mg Calc. *POINTS* value: *0.*

Sweet-and-Sour Barbecue Sauce

This aromatic sauce, so delicious on pork spareribs and chops, complements veal and turkey nicely too. It makes enough for about 1½ pounds of meat or poultry.

MAKES 12 SERVINGS

1 teaspoon canola oil
1 shallot, minced
1 garlic clove, minced
1 (8-ounce) can tomato sauce
¼ cup Marsala wine or
   apple juice

2 tablespoons wine vinegar or
   cider vinegar
2 teaspoons packed dark
   brown sugar
Hot pepper sauce, to taste
   (optional)

Heat the oil in a medium nonstick saucepan over medium heat. Add the shallot and garlic; cook until softened, stirring frequently, about 4 minutes. Add the tomato sauce, Marsala, vinegar, sugar, and pepper sauce (if using); bring to a boil. Reduce the heat and simmer, stirring occasionally, about 10 minutes.

Let the mixture cool about 10 minutes, then cover and refrigerate until ready to use, up to 3 days.

PER SERVING (generous 2 tablespoons): 18 Cal, 0 g Fat, 0 g Sat Fat, 0 g Trans Fat, 0 mg Chol, 124 mg Sod, 3 g Carb, 0 g Fib, 0 g Prot, 5 mg Calc. **POINTS** value: **0.**

✓ Simple Red Bell Pepper Sauce

This stunning red sauce is often used in restaurants to drizzle around the food on the plate. But not only does it look good, it tastes delicious, with a hint of sweetness and a little spicy kick from the cayenne. Use it to serve with grilled chicken, fish, or summer vegetables.

MAKES 4 SERVINGS 🥕

- **7 red bell peppers**
- **¼ cup water**
- **1 tablespoon + 1 teaspoon balsamic vinegar**

- **2 teaspoons olive oil**
- **4 garlic cloves, minced**
- **⅛ teaspoon cayenne or hot pepper sauce**

Spray the grill rack with nonstick spray; prepare the grill for a medium fire using the direct method (see page 81).

Place the bell peppers on the grill rack and grill, turning frequently with tongs as needed, until the skin is charred on all sides, about 10 minutes. Place the peppers in a heavy paper bag or large covered bowl; let stand about 20 minutes.

Working over a large bowl, carefully remove the charred skin, seeds, and stems from the peppers. Chop the peppers and place them in a blender or food processor along with any juices from the peppers. Pour in the water, vinegar, oil, garlic, and cayenne; puree until smooth. Transfer the sauce to a medium bowl; cover and refrigerate until ready to use, up to 1 week.

PER SERVING (about ½ cup): 81 Cal, 3 g Fat, 0 g Sat Fat, 0 g Trans Fat, 0 mg Chol, 5 mg Sod, 15 g Carb, 2 g Fib, 2 g Prot, 24 mg Calc. *POINTS* value: *1.*

 Jalapeño Green Sauce

This flavorful sauce is ideal on beef—in fact, it's the key ingredient in our Argentine Brisket (page 32). It's also delicious with grilled red snapper or chicken cutlets. For fresh, sparkling flavor, avoid making the sauce more than 6 hours before you plan to serve it.

MAKES 24 SERVINGS

½ cup coarsely chopped
   fresh cilantro
½ cup coarsely chopped fresh
   flat-leaf parsley
¼ cup coarsely chopped scallions
   (include some green parts)
¼ cup water

¼ cup red- or white-wine vinegar
1 tablespoon olive oil
2 medium garlic cloves, peeled
2 small jalapeño peppers,
   seeded (wear gloves to
   prevent irritation)
½ teaspoon salt

Combine the cilantro, parsley, scallions, water, vinegar, oil, garlic, jalapeños, and salt in a food processor or blender; process until smooth. Transfer to a serving bowl and refrigerate, covered, at least 2 hours to blend the flavors, or up to 6 hours.

PER SERVING (1 tablespoon): 7 Cal, 1 g Fat, 0 g Sat Fat, 0 g Trans Fat, 0 mg Chol, 50 mg Sod, 0 g Carb, 0 g Fib, 0 g Prot, 3 mg Calc. **POINTS** value: **0.**

Tex-Mex Barbecue Sauce

Barbecuing burgers, ribs, or chicken? Here's a hearty sauce, great for brushing on the meat toward the end of grilling or serving alongside. Tomato puree will yield a smooth sauce while crushed tomatoes, a chunkier one. The sauce will keep in the refrigerator for about a week.

MAKES 8 SERVINGS

2 teaspoons canola oil

1 onion, chopped

3 cups canned tomato puree or crushed tomatoes

3 tablespoons packed dark brown sugar

4 garlic cloves, crushed

1 teaspoon chili powder

1 teaspoon dry mustard

½ teaspoon salt

¼ teaspoon cayenne

2 tablespoons white-wine vinegar

Hot pepper sauce, to taste

Heat the oil in a medium nonstick saucepan over medium heat. Add the onion and cook, stirring frequently, until translucent, 4–5 minutes. Add the tomato puree, sugar, garlic, chili powder, mustard, salt, and cayenne; bring to a boil. Reduce the heat to low and simmer, covered, stirring occasionally, until thickened, about 1 hour.

Just before using, stir in the vinegar and pepper sauce.

PER SERVING (5 tablespoons): 80 Cal, 1 g Fat, 0 g Sat Fat, 0 g Trans Fat, 0 mg Chol, 528 mg Sod, 17 g Carb, 2 g Fib, 2 g Prot, 29 mg Calc. *POINTS* value: *1.*

Parsley-Basil Pesto

Similar to a traditional basil pesto, but with fresh parsley and a hint of fresh thyme added, this pesto is different and intriguing. It's terrific with hot cooked pasta of course, but try it too with grilled chicken or fish.

MAKES 4 SERVINGS

- ¾ cup lightly packed flat-leaf parsley leaves
- ¾ cup lightly packed fresh basil leaves
- 1 tablespoon fresh thyme leaves
- ½ teaspoon salt
- ¼ teaspoon freshly ground pepper

- 1 garlic clove, quartered
- 2 tablespoons chopped walnuts
- 3 tablespoons reduced-sodium chicken broth
- 1 tablespoon fresh lemon juice
- 1 teaspoon extra-virgin olive oil
- 2 tablespoons freshly grated Parmesan cheese

Combine the parsley, basil, thyme, salt, pepper, and garlic, and pepper in a food processor or blender; pulse until very finely chopped. Add the walnuts and process until the nuts are finely chopped.

With the motor running, pour in the broth; process until the mixture is smooth. Add the lemon juice, oil, and cheese; process again until smooth. Cover and refrigerate until ready to use, up to 2 days.

PER SERVING (2½ tablespoons): 81 Cal, 7 g Fat, 1 g Sat Fat, 0 g Trans Fat, 2 mg Chol, 363 mg Sod, 3 g Carb, 1 g Fib, 3 g Prot, 82 mg Calc. **POINTS** value: **2.**

Sweet Coriander Glaze

You don't need much of this zesty glaze—to brush on chicken, fish, or shrimp at the end of grilling—to add tremendous flavor. This recipe makes enough for about 1 pound of chicken or fish.

MAKES 4 SERVINGS 🌶 🕐 🥕

Grated zest of 1 lime
¼ cup fresh lime juice
2 tablespoons honey

¼ teaspoon coriander seeds,
crushed

Combine the lime zest, lime juice, honey, and coriander in a small bowl. Cover and refrigerate until ready to use, up to 2–3 days.

PER SERVING (1½ tablespoons): 36 Cal, 0 g Fat, 0 g Sat Fat, 0 g Trans Fat, 0 mg Chol, 4 mg Sod, 10 g Carb, 0 g Fib, 0 g Prot, 5 mg Calc. *POINTS* value: *1.*

TIP Crushing coriander seeds releases their flavor. To crush, place the seeds between two sheets of wax paper and pound them gently with a wooden mallet or the side of a chef's knife.

 Mango Relish

Fresh sweet mango, red onion, and ripe tomato make this relish beautiful to look at, while fresh jalapeño and lime juice pack it with tart, peppery flavor. Serve it alongside any grilled meat, chicken, or fish—it's especially delicious with Indian-Spiced Pork Chops (page 52).

MAKES 4 SERVINGS

1 large mango, peeled, pitted, and diced (about 1½cups)

¾ cup diced red onion

¾ cup diced seeded ripe tomato

1 tablespoon + 1 teaspoon minced jalapeño or serrano chile pepper (wear gloves to prevent irritation)

2 teaspoons fresh lime juice

¼ teaspoon salt

Combine the mango, onion, tomato, chile pepper, lime juice, and salt in a medium bowl; stir well. Let the mixture stand at least 1 hour before serving to blend the flavors. Or, cover and refrigerate until ready to use, up to 2 days.

PER SERVING (½ cup): 60 Cal, 0 g Fat, 0 g Sat Fat, 0 g Trans Fat, 0 mg Chol, 153 mg Sod, 15 g Carb, 2 g Fib, 1 g Prot, 15 mg Calc. *POINTS* value: *1*.

TIP Serrano chile peppers are small pointed chiles with a strong hot flavor. Younger green peppers are hotter than the mature red ones. They can be found in Latino grocery stores and some supermarkets. To avoid burns or irritation, wear gloves when handling serrano or jalapeño peppers, and wash hands immediately afterward.

FROM TOP, CLOCKWISE, MANGO RELISH, INDIAN-STYLE PEACH CHUTNEY, PAGE 207, AND PROVENÇAL RELISH, PAGE 206

☑ Provençal Relish

This unique orange-and-olive relish boasts flavors reminiscent of the south of France. It is a perfect accompaniment to grilled chicken or a firm-fleshed fish such as swordfish or tuna.

MAKES 4 SERVINGS

2 cups navel orange sections

12 large kalamata olives, pitted and diced

¼ cup + 2 tablespoons minced fresh parsley

1 tablespoon fresh thyme leaves

Combine the orange, olives, parsley, and thyme in a medium bowl. Let stand 1 hour before serving. Or cover and refrigerate until ready to use, up to 2 days.

PER SERVING (⅓ cup): 60 Cal, 2 g Fat, 0 g Sat Fat, 0 g Trans Fat, 0 mg Chol, 118 mg Sod, 12 g Carb, 3 g Fib, 1 g Pro, 58 mg Calc. *POINTS* value: *1.*

Indian-Style Peach Chutney

Chutneys, we know, are great with curried dishes, but try this rich and flavorful condiment to spice up any grilled meat, particularly pork or chicken.

MAKES 4 SERVINGS

 1 teaspoon extra-virgin olive oil
 1 onion, thinly sliced
 4 garlic cloves, minced
 4 fresh peaches sliced
    (about 2 cups)
 ½ cup cider vinegar
 ¼ cup packed brown sugar

 2 tablespoons raisins
 1-2 tablespoons thinly sliced
    seeded jalapeño pepper (wear
    gloves to prevent irritation)
 ⅛ teaspoon ground ginger
    Pinch ground cloves

Heat the oil in a medium nonstick saucepan over medium-high heat. Add the onion and cook, stirring constantly, until translucent, 6–8 minutes.

Add the garlic and cook, stirring, about 1 minute. Add the peaches, vinegar, sugar, raisins, jalapeño, ginger, and cloves; bring to a boil. Reduce the heat and simmer, stirring occasionally, about 50 minutes. Remove from the heat and let cool. Cover and refrigerate until ready to use, up to 2 weeks.

PER SERVING (about ½ cup): 137 Cal, 1 g Fat, 0 g Sat Fat, 0 g Trans Fat, 33 mg Chol, 8 mg Sod, 33 g Carb, 3 g Fib, 1 g Prot, 34 mg Calc. *POINTS* value: *2.*

☑ Ginger Onions

It takes time to caramelize onions to a perfect deep golden brown, rich and sweet in flavor. Start with large, sweet Vidalia onions if you can get them, but Bermuda or Spanish onions are good too. Fresh ginger gives a delicious twist to this naturally sweet condiment, making it perfect with grilled fish or chicken, or turkey burgers.

MAKES 4 SERVINGS 🥕

2 teaspoons olive oil
2 Vidalia onions, thinly sliced
   (about 4 cups)
¼ cup water

2 teaspoons slivered peeled
   fresh ginger
¼ teaspoon salt
1 teaspoon cider vinegar

Heat the oil in a large nonstick skillet over medium heat. Add the onions and water; cook, uncovered, stirring frequently, until the onions just begin to color, about 12 minutes.

Add the ginger and salt. Continue cooking, stirring frequently, until the onions are sweet and a deep brown color, about 30 minutes. Stir in the vinegar and serve at once. Or refrigerate, covered, for up to 1 week.

PER SERVING (3 tablespoons): 64 Cal, 2 g Fat, 0 g Sat Fat, 0 g Trans Fat, 0 mg Chol, 151 mg Sod, 10 g Carb, 2 g Fib, 1 g Prot, 23 mg Calc. **_POINTS_** value: **_1._**

☑ Grill-Roasted Garlic

Garlic roasted on a grill or in the oven can be used as an alternative to olive oil or butter when you're serving crusty French or Italian bread. Or, use it to perk up mashed potatoes, sauces, even soups by stirring in a few teaspoons of the garlic. The roasting mellows the garlic's flavor, leaving it subtle and sweet. It will keep for up to 3 weeks, well wrapped, in the refrigerator.

MAKES 4 SERVINGS 🥕

4 small garlic heads

Prepare the grill for a medium fire using the direct method (see page 81).

Wrap each garlic head in 4 layers of heavy-duty foil.

Place the garlic on the grill rack and grill until soft, 40–45 minutes. Remove the foil and let the garlic cool slightly. Squeeze the roasted garlic pulp out of the papery skins into a small bowl.

PER SERVING (1 tablespoon): 45 Cal, 0 g Fat, 0 g Sat Fat, 0 g Trans Fat, 0 mg Chol, 5 mg Sod, 10 g Carb, 1 g Fib, 2 g Prot, 54 mg Calc. *POINTS* value: *1.*

TIP If you prefer, you can roast garlic on a baking sheet in a 350°F oven for about 50 minutes.

Light and
Fruity Endings

Charred Bananas with Sweet Lime Sauce

This sweet-and-piquant dessert is sure to be a favorite. For a special "grilled banana split," serve it with a ½-cup scoop of fat-free frozen yogurt and increase the **POINTS** value by 2.

MAKES 4 SERVINGS 🕐

1 tablespoon + 1 teaspoon packed brown sugar

2 teaspoons fresh lime juice

½ teaspoon grated peeled fresh ginger

2 bananas, split lengthwise

Spray the grill rack with nonstick spray; prepare the grill for a hot fire using the direct method (see page 81).

To make the ginger sauce, combine the sugar, lime juice, and ginger in a small bowl. Set aside.

Place the bananas on the grill rack and grill until lightly browned, about 3 minutes on each side. Transfer the bananas to individual serving plates and drizzle each with the ginger sauce. Serve warm.

PER SERVING (½ banana and 1 teaspoon sauce): 69 Cal, 0 g Fat, 0 g Sat Fat, 0 g Trans Fat, 0 mg Chol, 2 mg Sod, 18 g Carb, 1 g Fib, 1 g Prot, 7 mg Calc. **POINTS** value: *1.*

TIP The bananas become a bit soft as they grill, so try using an extra-wide spatula to turn them more easily. Use bananas that are firm with no brown spots as they will hold up better.

Drunken Cantaloupe

Here's a delicious, summery dessert, which makes a beautiful finish to just about any grilled dinner—beef, pork, chicken, or fish.

MAKES 4 SERVINGS

1 small ripe cantaloupe, seeded and cut into 1-inch chunks

2 tablespoons fresh orange juice

2 tablespoons orange-flavored liqueur, such as Cointreau or Grand Marnier

Spray the grill rack with nonstick spray; prepare the grill for a medium fire using the direct method (see page 81). If you are using wooden skewers, soak them in water for 30 minutes.

Thread the cantaloupe chunks onto 6 (12-inch) metal or wooden skewers, leaving about 1/8 inch between each chunk. Place the skewers at the edge of the grill rack and grill, turning often, until the cantaloupe is warmed through, but not charred, about 4 minutes. Remove the cantaloupe from the skewers and place in a serving bowl.

Combine the orange juice and liqueur in a small bowl; drizzle over the hot cantaloupe and serve at once.

PER SERVING (1/4 of cantaloupe and 1 tablespoon drizzle): 64 Cal, 0 g Fat, 0 g Sat Fat, 0 g Trans Fat, 0 mg Chol, 10 mg Sod, 13 g Carb, 1 g Fib, 1 g Prot, 13 mg Calc. **POINTS** value: *1.*

TIP This dish also works beautifully as a side dish, especially with pork or chicken. Instead of the orange juice and liqueur, combine 2 tablespoons of fresh lime juice with a pinch each of salt and cayenne, then drizzle it over the grilled melon.

☑ Grilled Grapefruit and Orange Sections

This colorful and refreshing combination is a perfect, light ending to a hearty grilled dinner. Or try it as an appetizing starter, or as an accompaniment to grilled chicken, pork, or fish.

MAKES 4 SERVINGS

1 grapefruit, peeled and sectioned

1 large navel orange, peeled and sectioned

4 sprigs fresh mint

Prepare the grill for a medium fire using the direct method (see page 81). Spray a grill basket with nonstick spray.

Arrange the grapefruit and orange sections in a single layer in the grill basket; place the grill basket on the grill. Grill until the fruit is warmed through but not charred, about 2 minutes on each side. Garnish with mint sprigs and serve at once.

PER SERVING (4 sections each grapefruit and orange): 36 Cal, 0 g Fat, 0 g Sat Fat, 0 g Trans Fat, 0 mg Chol, 1 mg Sod, 9 g Carb, 2 g Fib, 1 g Prot, 24 mg Calc. *POINTS* value: *0.*

CINNAMON-SPICED PEACHES

Cinnamon-Spiced Peaches

What could be easier? The peaches are sprinkled with sugar and spices, wrapped in a foil package, and cooked on the side of the grill while you grill the entrée. The added bonus is—no pan to clean. Serve with a small cinnamon twist or a biscotti and increase the **POINTS** value by 1.

MAKES 6 SERVINGS

2 teaspoons packed brown sugar
2 teaspoons canola oil
½ teaspoon vanilla extract
¼ teaspoon cinnamon

¼ teaspoon rum extract
Pinch ground allspice
6 fresh ripe peaches

Prepare the grill for a medium fire using the direct method (see page 81).

Combine sugar, oil, vanilla, cinnamon, rum extract, and allspice in a small bowl.

Slice each peach in half vertically and remove the pit. Place the peach halves, cut-side up, in two rows in the center of a double thickness of foil. With a pastry brush, spread the cut side of each peach half liberally with the oil-and-spice mixture, letting some collect in the center of each half. Make a packet by bringing 2 sides of the foil up to meet in the center and pressing the edges together in 2 (½-inch) folds. Then fold the edges of each end together in 2 (½-inch) folds. Crimp the edges together to seal, allowing room for the packet to expand as it grills.

Place the packet on the grill rack and grill until the peaches are soft, 15–20 minutes. Remove the packet from the grill and open carefully to avoid the hot steam. Serve warm.

PER SERVING (2 peach halves): 63 Cal, 2 g Fat, 0 g Sat Fat, 0 g Trans Fat, 0 mg Chol, 1 mg Sod, 13 g Carb, 2 g Fib, 1 g Prot, 8 mg Calc. **POINTS** value: **1.**

TIP If you prefer, substitute nectarines for the peaches.

Maple-Glazed Pineapple

Glazed with maple syrup, rum, and cinnamon, then grilled, this fresh pineapple makes a delicious dessert served warm or at room temperature. Try with a scoop of lemon or mango sorbet. It is also a refreshing accompaniment to grilled ham, chicken, or turkey. Store any leftovers in the refrigerator—they'll taste great over breakfast cereal in the morning.

MAKES 6 SERVINGS

½ cup maple syrup

1 teaspoon cinnamon

½ teaspoon rum extract

1 (3½-pound) ripe pineapple

Spray the grill rack with nonstick spray; prepare the grill for a medium fire using the direct method (see page 81).

Combine the syrup, cinnamon, and rum extract in a small bowl.

To prepare the pineapple, using a sharp chef's knife, slice off the crown and the bottom of the pineapple. Place the pineapple upright on a cutting board and slice off the outer skin. With a sharp paring knife or the end of a vegetable peeler, remove the "eyes." Halve the pineapple lengthwise. With a sharp knife, cut away and discard the core with a Brush the halves with the syrup mixture.

Place the pineapple halves on the grill rack and grill, turning frequently with tongs and basting often with the syrup mixture, until the pineapple is glazed and lightly browned, 40–45 minutes.

Remove pineapple halves from grill and cut each half into 9 (½-inch) slices.

PER SERVING (3 slices pineapple): 139 Cal, 1 g Fat, 0 g Sat Fat, 0 g Trans Fat, 0 mg Chol, 4 mg Sod, 35 g Carb, 2 g Fib, 1 g Prot, 32 mg Calc. *POINTS* value: *2.*

MAPLE-GLAZED
PINEAPPLE

DRY AND LIQUID MEASUREMENT EQUIVALENTS

If you are converting the recipes in this book to metric measurements, use the following chart as a guide.

TEASPOONS	TABLESPOONS	CUPS	FLUID OUNCES
3 teaspoons	1 tablespoon		½ fluid ounce
6 teaspoons	2 tablespoons	⅛ cup	1 fluid ounce
8 teaspoons	2 tablespoons plus 2 teaspoons	⅙ cup	
12 teaspoons	4 tablespoons	¼ cup	2 fluid ounces
15 teaspoons	5 tablespoons	⅓ cup minus 1 teaspoon	
16 teaspoons	5 tablespoons plus 1 teaspoon	⅓ cup	
18 teaspoons	6 tablespoons	¼ cup plus 2 tablespoons	3 fluid ounces
24 teaspoons	8 tablespoons	½ cup	4 fluid ounces
30 teaspoons	10 tablespoons	½ cup plus 2 tablespoons	5 fluid ounces
32 teaspoons	10 tablespoons plus 2 teaspoons	⅔ cup	
36 teaspoons	12 tablespoons	¾ cup	6 fluid ounces
42 teaspoons	14 tablespoons	1 cup minus 2 tablespoons	7 fluid ounces
45 teaspoons	15 tablespoons	1 cup minus 1 tablespoon	
48 teaspoons	16 tablespoons	1 cup	8 fluid ounces

VOLUME

¼ teaspoon	1 milliliter
½ teaspoon	2 milliliters
1 teaspoon	5 milliliters
1 tablespoon	15 milliliters
2 tablespoons	30 milliliters
3 tablespoons	45 milliliters
¼ cup	60 milliliters
⅓ cup	80 milliliters
½ cup	120 milliliters
⅔ cup	160 milliliters
¾ cup	175 milliliters
1 cup	240 milliliters
1 quart	950 milliliters

LENGTH

1 inch	25 millimeters
1 inch	2.5 centimeters

OVEN TEMPERATURE

250°F	120°C	400°F	200°C
275°F	140°C	425°F	220°C
300°F	150°C	450°F	230°C
325°F	160°C	475°F	250°C
350°F	180°C	500°F	260°C
375°F	190°C	525°F	270°C

WEIGHT

1 ounce	30 grams
¼ pound	120 grams
½ pound	240 grams
1 pound	480 grams

NOTE: Measurement of less than ⅛ teaspoon is considered a dash or a pinch. Metric volume measurements are approximate.

Index

POINTS value Recipe Index

Turkey Spiedini, 78

Veal Chops with Honey-Mustard Glaze, 46

Warm Grilled Potatoes and Sweet Onions, 162

Zucchini and Goat Cheese on Flatbread, 184

4 POINTS value

Argentine Brisket, 32

Bacon-Wrapped Chicken Thighs, 69

Beer-Marinated Grilled Cornish Hens, 83

Charred Eggplant and Tomato with Goat Cheese, 126

Chicken with Lemon, Ginger, and Basil, 67

Cod Steaks Grilled in Grape Leaves, 103

Cornish Hens with Sweet and Fruity Glaze, 85

Creamy Corn Chowder, 22

Duck Breasts with Spicy Apricot Glaze, 87

Grilled Calamari with Mustard Dressing, 111

Grilled Pork Kebabs, 48

Grilled Turkey Roulade, 76

Herb and Mustard Beef Tenderloin, 30

Indian-Spiced Pork Chops, 52

Moroccan-Spiced Beef Kebabs, 42

Pita Breads with Thyme, 188

Pork Souvlaki with Cucumber-Yogurt Sauce, 49

Rice, Carrot, and Zucchini Salad, 153

Shrimp, Hummus, and Red Pepper Pizza, 186

Southern Corn Bread in a Skillet, 191

Speedy Pesto Scallops, 110

Summer Vegetable Pasta Salad, 154

T-Bone Steak with Horseradish Sauce, 33

Thyme-Seasoned Grouper, 105

Tuna Niçoise Salad, 150

Whole Grilled Chicken with Rosemary, 62

5 POINTS value

Barbecued Beef on a Bun, 39

Coastal Pizza, 179

Curry-Marinated Chicken Kebabs, 68

Duck with Sweet-and-Sour Cabbage, 88

Grilled Mustard-Crumbed Flank Steak with Vegetables, 37

Grilled Radicchio and Shiitake Pizza, 180

Grilled Shrimp, Snow Pea, and Rice Salad, 148

Grilled Steak and Potato Salad, 151

Herb-Marinated Quails, 89

Lime-Tamari Grilled Swordfish, 98

Marinated Flank Steak with Cherry Tomato Salad, 35

Smoked Turkey, Grilled Onion, and Tomato Pizza, 175

Spicy Salmon Steaks with Tarragon Sauce, 92

Spicy Sausage and White Bean Pizza, 181

Steak Roulade, 38

Swordfish Kebabs with Spicy Nut Sauce, 97

Tandoori Lamb, 53

Turkey Cutlets with Cranberry Salsa, 79

Walnut-Crusted Lamb Chops, 57

Zesty London Broil, 34

6 POINTS value

Asian Tuna with Water Chestnuts on a Stick, 96

California Sausage-and-Pepper Pizza, 176

Chicken Teriyaki with Udon, 70

Grilled Canadian Bacon and Pear Pizza, 178

Grilled Chicken Cordon Bleu, 66

Greek Chicken with Pitas and Tzatziki, 65

Herbed Beef Burgers, 45

Lamb Chops with Tomato Chutney, 56

Pork and Poblano Pepper Pizza, 168

Pork Cutlets with Apple-Onion Topping, 50

Red Snapper with Corn-Raisin Relish, 99

Steak Lovers' Grilled Pizza, 170

7 POINTS value

Chicken, Corn, and Manchego Pizza, 171

Easy Asian-Marinated Halibut, 104

Grilled Chicken and Avocado Quesadillas, 73

Herbed Duck and Tomato Pizza, 173

Quick-Grilled Bluefish Fillets, 106

Sage Chicken and Pepper Pizza, 172

8 POINTS value

Grilled Tuna with Corn and Pea Sauté, 95

NOTES